# book *of* faith
## Advent Reflections
### Making All Things New

# book *of* faith
## Advent Reflections
### Making All Things New

Kae Evensen
Carolyn Coon Mowchan
Margaret A. Krych
Peter W. Marty
Debbie Trafton O'Neal

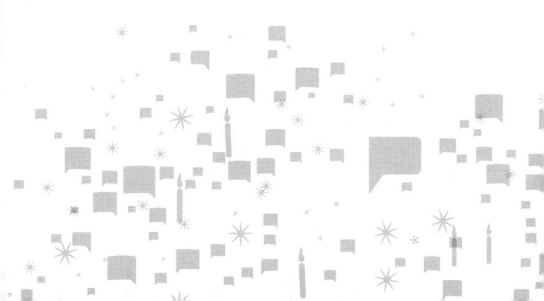

BOOK OF FAITH ADVENT REFLECTIONS
Making All Things New

Unless otherwise identified, Scripture quotations are from the New Revised Standard Version Bible, copyright © 1989 by the Division of Christian Education of the National Council of the Churches of Christ in the USA. Used by permission. All rights reserved.

Citations from ELW are from *Evangelical Lutheran Worship*, copyright © 2006 Evangelical Lutheran Church in America (Minneapolis: Augsburg Fortress).

For information on the Book of Faith initiative and Book of Faith resources, go to www.bookoffaith.org.

Book of Faith is an initiative of the
**Evangelical Lutheran Church in America**
God's work. Our hands.

Cover design: Joe Vaughan, Running Design Group
Interior composition: PerfecType, Nashville, TN
Technical art: Tory Herman

ISBN 978-1-4514-0261-2

The paper used in this publication meets the minimum requirements of American National Standard for Information Sciences—Permanence of Paper for Printed Library Materials, ANSI Z329.48-1984.

Manufactured in the U.S.A.

14    13    12    11    1    2    3    4    5    6    7    8    9    10

# Contents

# Introduction

For centuries, the season of Advent has been a holy time of reflection and preparation for the celebration of Jesus' birth. For many of us, however, Advent has become one of the most hectic times of the year. We deck the halls, send Christmas cards or e-cards, shop for gifts, wrap the gifts, bake and cook, attend special events, and travel to spend time with family and friends, all the while wondering how we'll get everything done in four short weeks. When the countdown to Christmas is over and the presents are all ripped open, we're too run-down and exhausted to welcome the Prince of Peace into our hearts and lives.

While we're so focused on what we're doing and what still needs to be done, it's easy to overlook what God is doing. And God is up to something, during Advent and Christmas and each day of every season. God is not only busy, but getting things done, in us and through us and in the world. God is at work—renewing, redeeming, refreshing, reenergizing, reinventing—to make all things new!

*Advent Reflections: Making All Things New* celebrates what God is up to. Through daily reflections, weekly Bible studies, and hands-on activities, you will explore how God renews all things, particularly our stories, our days, our spirits, and our ways. God redeems and renews our stories and the world's story, and forever weaves them into God's story. God takes our days out of the "same old, same old" and gives us a fresh start each morning, calling us to serve Jesus and others and leading us toward promise. By grace through faith, God forgives us and completely renews our spirits, our very selves. God makes us new creations, giving us not only new ways, but new life in Christ. This work of making all things new is God's gracious gift to us and to the world.

*Advent Reflections* is a Book of Faith resource. In 2007 the Evangelical Lutheran Church in America (ELCA) affirmed the centrality of the Bible to Christian life and faith, and at the same time recognized the reality of biblical illiteracy in the church. This resulted in the Book of Faith initiative, which invites us to open Scripture and join the conversation. By looking at the Bible through different lenses—historical, literary, Lutheran, and devotional—we can enter into a dialogue with God's Word in ways that lead to deeper understanding and spiritual growth. The emphasis in this book is on the devotional lens, but the other lenses are used to provide insights into Scripture as well. As a Book of Faith resource, *Advent Reflections* offers opportunities to open Scripture, look at it through different lenses, and join conversations with the Bible, with friends or family, with a small group, and, ultimately, with God.

# How to Use This Book

Start this book on the first Sunday in Advent (four Sundays before Christmas), if possible. Put it in a prominent place in your home, purse, backpack, or briefcase, so you'll be reminded to use it every day. Use the daily reflections, weekly Bible studies, and activities during the Advent season to explore and celebrate God's work of making all things new.

## Advent Reflections

This section guides you in a daily devotional time with a reflection, questions, and a prayer for every day in Advent. (See pp. 13–69.) Have a Bible handy each day so that you can read the text and then the reflection. Spend a few moments thinking about the "Questions to Ponder." Close your devotional time with the prayer, perhaps followed by a prayer of your own or a few moments of silence.

You can connect this devotional time with things that are already part of your daily routine. Here are a few suggestions for doing this. Ask others for their ideas as well. Read the Bible text, reflection, and prayer during a meal, coffee break, or bus ride. Consider the "Questions to Ponder" as you take a walk, wait in line, or spend some quiet time thinking and praying. When you are with friends and family members, talk about what you are reading and learning. Open your heart to the Spirit's work of renewal.

## Bible Studies

Four Bible studies, one for each week in Advent, highlight the four main themes used in the daily reflections: Renew Our Stories, Renew Our Days, Renew Our Spirits, Renew Our Ways (see pp. 71–79). Use these Bible studies once a week on your own, with a friend or family member, in a small group that already exists, or in a new group formed with other people who are reading this book. If you are in a small group using the Bible studies in this book, be sure to take time for the daily reflections as well.

## Activities

The Activities section (pp. 81–101) provides many hands-on ways for families with younger children to celebrate the Advent season. You may want to scan this entire section before Advent begins and pick out one or two activities for each week, or simply choose activities as the season goes along. Either way, focus on what is most doable and meaningful for your family, not on finishing every activity provided.

The Faith Flag Banner is an activity that you can begin at the start of the season and build on each week. Hanging over a mantel, in a doorway, or along a banister, this banner will help you celebrate Advent and remember that God makes all things new.

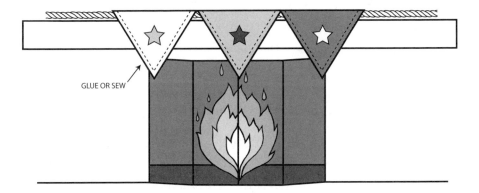

GLUE OR SEW

## Our Writers

### Week 1 Reflections and Bible Study: Renew Our Stories

*Kae Evensen* is a pastor at Mercy Seat Lutheran Church in northeast Minneapolis, Minnesota. She works with her amazing pastoral colleague Mark Stenberg and lives with her wonderful family, Marty, Jimmy, and Emily.

### Week 2 Reflections and Bible Study: Renew Our Days

*Carolyn Coon Mowchan* is a pastor whose work has been seen in devotions, Bible studies, curriculum, and *The Lutheran* and *Partners* magazines. She has written two books in the Lutheran Voices series: *Connecting with God in a Disconnected World* (coauthored with Damian Anthony Vraniak, 2003) and *Holy Purpose* (2007). She lives with her husband, Will, also a pastor, in the north woods of Wisconsin.

### Week 3 Reflections and Bible Study: Renew Our Spirits

*Margaret A. Krych* is an ordained pastor and published author who served as a faculty member and associate dean of graduate education at the Lutheran Theological Seminary at Philadelphia. As the Charles F. Norton professor emerita of Christian Education and Theology, she continues teaching occasional courses at the seminary. She lives in Pennsylvania with her husband, Arden, also a retired pastor.

### Week 4 Reflections and Bible Study: Renew Our Ways

*Peter W. Marty* is senior pastor of St. Paul Lutheran Church, Davenport, Iowa. He preaches and speaks frequently at colleges, churches, and conferences across the country. Marty is the author of *The Anatomy of Grace* (Augsburg Fortress, 2008), among many writings. From 2004 to 2009, he was host of the national radio broadcast *Grace Matters*. The Academy of Parish Clergy named him Parish Pastor of the Year in 2010.

## Activities

*Debbie Trafton O'Neal* is an author, educator, and consultant who lives in the Seattle, Washington, area. She has written more than fifty books for children, families, and educators, and has developed, written, and edited curriculum for more than twenty-five years. Creative, hands-on experiences are her favorite ways to teach and learn.

# Advent Reflections

# Week 1: Renew Our Stories

## Day 1: Sunday

### What Are We Waiting For?

Mark 13:32-37

> 🗨 *Key Verse:* Therefore, keep awake—for you do not know when the master of the house will come, in the evening, or at midnight, or at cockcrow, or at dawn, or else he may find you asleep when he comes suddenly. Mark 13:35-36

These days, it's hard to figure out what's urgent and what's not; all our stories feel that way. Yet this is the season of Advent, an urgent season full of Bible texts that bump up against our stories. Advent is the season of hope, of waiting, of expectation, of longing, and yet it is also the season when we read and hear texts that push at our hearts and rack our brains because often they seem to come up short on promise. So we comb through them carefully, trying not to snuff out their hope, while still allowing them to breathe out their lovely, revelatory life.

This passage from the Gospel of Mark is one of these difficult texts. We try to tame it by corralling it, so maybe it won't seem so foreign and disruptive. Yet in this Advent season, the rawness of Mark 13:32-37 comes to us bearing a truth, a passion, and a beckoning, and we don't need to try to manufacture any compulsion to fix it.

What we tend to forget is that beneath this difficult text is the *who.* Who is asking us to wait, who is asking us to keep awake? When we shift the focus to who is speaking, we discover that we don't have to worry so much, that our urgent needs are covered, that we can let go, because the hard work is already done. We find the heavy lifting is over. There is good news here because of the one who speaks, Jesus Christ. Our story—all our stories—already have been folded into his promise.

Because of Christ and his crazy, amazing love for us, because of who he is, our stories are now his. We do not need to worry; we do not need to beat ourselves up to meet this text's demands. Christ has already met them, and the Christ upon whom we wait is the same Christ who will soon come to us in the form of a child, the same Christ who goes to the cross, the same Christ who walks away from the tomb before the disciples have a chance to rub the sleep from their eyes. Beneath the difficult words of Mark 13:32-37 is a greater promise, a deeper story—a promise we are merely given, a story that not only bears our past but keeps us wide-eyed and awake, to give us faith and to recognize real hope.

### Questions to Ponder

- What keeps you awake at night? What is your greatest worry?
- In what ways is it helpful for you to know that you and your loved ones are already taken into God's story, a story brimming with promise?

### Prayer

Gracious Christ, it is your deepest joy to gather our story into yours. Keep us awake to your promises, promises that renew us each moment, each day. Amen.

## Day 2: Monday

### A Promise Given

Micah 4:1-5

> *Key Verse:* We will walk in the name of the Lord our God forever and ever. Micah 4:5b

Part of my story and your story, as well as the whole human story, is that we are a broken people deeply in need of God's grace. No corner of our world remains untouched by suffering, violence, or death. Tragedy refuses the boundaries we try to impose upon it. Sometimes it seems like our lives and even the world have hit rock bottom and there is no hope.

A small-town kid, the prophet Micah set off for the big city of Jerusalem during one of the most turbulent periods in Israel's history. War was flaring and the country was divided. Anger raged. For generations, things appeared not only bleak but outright hopeless. But Micah saw beyond his time, beyond the city walls, even beyond history itself, to a God who longed to restore the people. Micah imagined a leader, a Messiah, who would come to restore the nations, changing the story from one of war and hopelessness to peace and prosperity, when the nations would "beat their swords into plowshares" (Micah 4:3).

We still cling to Micah's words of promise. Though we are a post-cross, post-resurrection people, we continue to live in a world that stretches our deeply cherished longings for peace. At times we might wonder, as Micah does, what this world is coming to, but like this strange country prophet, we also know that we have a God who will not let us go. We have a God who keeps promises. We have a God whose greatest joy is to enter into the very midst of our suffering, our sin, even our violence, to bring hope and peace. We have a God who delights in forgiveness, who rejoices in reconciliation, and who loves to raise the dead. This God is for all people and all nations, and this God is for you.

Our story, the world's story, and, yes, your story, are forever woven into God's. And the promise is: there will be peace, there will be restoration, there will be resurrection.

*Questions to Ponder*

- Think about a time when you felt hopeless about something, whether it was about your life, your community, or the world. How did your faith give you hope?
- God spoke to Micah, offering vision and promise in difficult times. How does God speak to you?

*Prayer*

Holy God, in our fragile lives, with our limited vision, often we find it difficult to imagine that your hope is real in this world. Give us a glimpse of your promise. Give us eyes to see your ongoing redemptive work, your work that makes all things new. Amen.

## Day 3: Tuesday

### A Bit More Than an Uh-oh, a Tad More Than an Oops

Psalm 79

> *Key Verse:* Help us, O God of our salvation, for the glory of your name; deliver us, and forgive our sins, for your name's sake.
> Psalm 79:9

Inside all our quirky human psyches is something that longs for forgiveness for things we've said or done—and things we didn't say or do. God already knows this about us and still wants to keep us around, and that allows us to talk about needing forgiveness as a shared reality. We don't need to keep this a secret. We don't have to pretend we are perfect or that life is perfect. This is a huge relief.

There are narrative threads woven throughout the biblical story. One of the most constant is our need for confession and forgiveness. It all starts, of course, with Adam and Eve. We soon discover that people we consider heroes in the Bible aren't that heroic after all. Many are in need of a good shot of repentance, just like the rest of us humans. The story tumbles right along like this, down through the generations, finally becoming our story too.

The writer of Psalm 79 speaks for the nation, for all of Jerusalem. Not only have individuals sinned; the whole nation has sinned and is in need of absolution. As the psalmist understands it, God is a personal God but doesn't merely reside inside the warm recesses of an individual's heart. No, this is a God who personally takes interest in God's people and in the world.

God takes this interest even further by entering the world's story through a child's story. This child is Jesus Christ, fully human and also fully divine. The grace is that all our stories are taken into this child's. It's a stunning story really, transcendent and yet completely down-to-earth. It redeems our present story and our future story—and not just our story, but the world's, because God loves you, us, and the world.

In this season of Advent, we can take great comfort. We are free to confess, to admit not only that we bumble, but that we are broken through and through. We are free to hear that we are not the first to be broken, nor will we be the last.

We are free to know that God does not measure with a yardstick or quid pro quo, but with mercy and compassion. God so loved the world and chose to weave Christ's story right into the heart of ours.

*Questions to Ponder*

- When you speak words of confession, in personal prayer or during confession in worship, what do you hope to feel?
- When have you seen something good come out of an experience that seemed irretrievably broken?

*Prayer*

Good and holy Christ, it is your delight to free us from all things that bind us. Forgive us and heal us this day. Knowing that we are deeply loved, set us on our way again. Amen.

## Day 4: Wednesday

### The Peace of Christ

Luke 21:34-38

> 💬 *Key Verse:* Every day he was teaching in the temple, and at night he would go out and spend the night on the Mount of Olives, as it was called. Luke 21:37

In Luke, right before the plot to kill Jesus is revealed, Jesus says, "Be on guard so that your hearts are not weighed down with dissipation and drunkenness and the worries of this life, and that day does not catch you unexpectedly, like a trap" (21:34-35a). This is right before the Passover Festival, the day a lamb would be sacrificed in honor of God, for freeing the Israelites from oppressive slavery in Egypt so many years before. If you were a first-century hearer of this text, you would notice the layers of meaning imposed upon Jesus' words. You would hear the heavy background music begin as you picture a familiar place, the Mount of Olives, where Jesus goes to pray, and remember the betrayal of Judas, and suddenly make connections between the meaning of Passover and what is about to unfold. As with any good story, the tension would build and you would be on the edge of your seat.

Some of this meaning probably is lost on us today, but we still can sense the growing tension. We know what it's like to wonder what's next. We've all sat next to our phones or computers, waiting, the tension building as time goes on. Will I get accepted to the college of my choice? Did I completely bomb that question in the job interview? What did the doctor discover on the MRI? When will that baby be born?

There is a growing tension, too, in this season of Advent, right in the midst of endless celebrations, to-do lists, and shopping. This is one of the busiest times of year—and for some of us, the most difficult and sorrowful. We are faced with our own longings, because our story does not necessarily mesh with the story of those around us. What are we waiting for in this season? Where can we find peace?

The story in Luke 21:34-38 is our story, for it tells us of a time when everyone is rushing around and getting ready for a celebration, while Christ's heart is weighed down with grief, and he takes time to pray. Yet this story is even more. Because of who Christ is, it inverts all our stories and turns them from mad dashes into calm hope, allowing us to stop and pray, wherever our Mount of Olives might be. Christ takes our limited, hectic stories into his and, in turn, gives us peace.

*Questions to Ponder*

- Imagine hearing the story of Christ for the first time. How would you react to it?
- During this Advent season, how might you create reminders that Christ comes to bring you peace?

*Prayer*

Holy Christ, you come into this season, into our lives, into our very days, to bring us your peace. May we enjoy your peace and share it with the people and world around us. Amen.

## Day 5: Thursday

### God's Love Is Certain

Hosea 6:1-6

> *Key Verse:* He will come to us like the showers, like the spring rains that water the earth. Hosea 6:3b

Hosea's prophecies begin with his personal life. Hosea, a heartbroken husband, grieves deeply over his wife's unfaithfulness, yet remains faithful to her. After each transgression, Hosea continues to proclaim his love for her. Hosea's prophecies to the nation, then, come from the very place of his most intimate grief: the people of Israel are like an unfaithful spouse, and God will not them go.

We are unfaithful to God, time and time again. We forget that everything in this world—our breath, our being, our loved ones—are all gifts from God. We tend to focus on ourselves and our problems. But the God we await in the Christ child is the same God of the Hebrew Bible, our Old Testament. This God loves to take care of us and assures us of forgiveness and life. God's faithfulness continues through time and every generation, over and over again, and begins anew with us. We can depend on God to be faithful, then, even when we are not. Though we forget God, God will not forget us.

As Hosea proclaims, all God longs for is our love in return. We do not need to jump through moral hoops or pietistic rituals. It sounds so simple, so absurd, but it is true; we are simply asked to trust that God's love for us is real, to lean on it in times of need, and to offer thanks in times of plenty.

Hosea compares God's love for us to spring rains upon the earth. What seems barren and gray, hopeless and forsaken, will soon blossom under this steadfast outpouring. Something new will emerge. And so it is for us. We wait, during these days in Advent, for the Christ child, a sign of hope and new life—the assurance that God will never forsake us or let us go. The Christ child is the most absurd and vulnerable of gifts, and yet the perfect gift of God's love for us and the world.

*Questions to Ponder*

- Think about a time in your life when you felt God had forgotten you. What, if anything, changed your perspective?
- God risked becoming vulnerable, both as a child and on the cross. How does this vulnerability speak to you about God's love?

*Prayer*

God of all ages, help us hear and gather confidence around this, that your love is the only certain thing in our lives. Amen.

## Day 6: Friday

### A God of Miracles

Acts 11:19-26

> *Key Verse:* The hand of the Lord was with them, and a great number became believers and turned to the Lord. Acts 11:21

Many of us are familiar with Jesus' miracles, such as turning water into wine at the wedding in Cana, healing ten lepers, and feeding the five thousand. We might pray for a miracle when a loved one is gravely ill, but for many of us this is playing our last card. How many people in our modern world believe in miracles?

The writer of Acts picks up where the Gospels end. Despite heartbreaking setbacks and failures, infighting, low turnout at worship services, and the deaths of Stephen and Barnabas, in Acts the Holy Spirit is clearly at work creating a new story, setting the foundation for what we know as church. With a ragtag bunch of believers and their uncertain mission plan, it is a miracle that this ship ever left port!

Yet, isn't that God? And isn't that how God works in the world? Out of the waste, the leftovers, out of the least of these, God creates hope and life. In Acts 11, the most unlikely thing is happening—the church in Antioch is growing beyond an almost entirely Jewish population to include non-Jews (Gentiles). In fact, a large number of church members in Antioch are Gentiles. This was unthinkable only a few years earlier when the first Jewish Christians started the church. It was unthinkable that a Jewish man might step into a non-Jewish home for worship. It was unthinkable that a Roman centurion, Cornelius, would become one of the most faithful disciples of the early church.

Yet, isn't that our God? Isn't it just like our God to do what we can't imagine, what we might consider unthinkable? Isn't it just like God to turn over our placid expectations and demure dreams? From the very first day, when God spoke light into being, God has been about miracles. And now, God still is working below and beneath what we imagine, doing the unthinkable, doing the miraculous.

Even now, as you're reading this, God is acting—working miracles in ways you could never imagine or expect. Even now, God is working in you, creating you anew each day, blessing you in the most tender of ways, and leading you toward promise. Even now, despite whatever setbacks you may face, or whatever hardship or sorrow might assail you, God is working in those places, for your life is the very material that God uses to bring hope and promise into the world.

## Questions to Ponder

- What is most discouraging for you right now? Imagine ways that God might redeem your discouragement and offer you hope.
- What sort of miracles have you witnessed? Did they happen suddenly or over time? How was God at work?

## Prayer

Holy Lord, it is your joy to take mourning and turn it to joy; grief, and turn it to hope; death, and turn it to life. Help us to see your work in our lives as well as in the world around us. Amen.

## *Day 7: Saturday*

## The Authority of Christ

Mark 11:27-33

🗨 *Key Verse:* By what authority are you doing these things? Mark 11:28

Throughout the Gospel of Mark, it seems like Jesus is trying to keep his story a secret. The Gospel writer tells us in the first verse of the first chapter that this is "the beginning of the good news of Jesus Christ, the Son of God." But few others in the Gospel know this. So we read Mark almost as a "whodunit," and the suspense lies in watching the characters figure it out. We might view ourselves as observers of the story but never really characters in it. However, the brilliance of Mark's unique narrative is that we think we're not part of the story—until the end of the Gospel.

We can easily be convinced that we are merely observers of a tale told more than two thousand years ago, whose main characters are long dead. But as the writer of Mark demonstrates, we are as much a part of God's story as the disciples around Jesus, as central to the story as those who first spoke it to us, and this story lingers for children yet to be. Our God is not just any god, a god who remains detached and far away in the heavens, but a God of relationship who longs to be in relationship with each person in this world. The Gospel writer even introduces Jesus in terms of relationship—the Son of God.

During these four weeks of Advent, we are drawn nearer to the center of God's story, the incarnation. We will soon celebrate what God is about through this Son made flesh, who though clothed in vulnerability and weakness bears all that is great and good. We are vulnerable and weak ourselves, but the riches of the Father are made ours through this child, the Son. And we are humbled. Like the first shepherds and kings who witnessed this event, we cannot imagine that our gifts are worthy for this one. But that's okay, because the Son, who has all authority over heaven and earth, joyfully comes to us, bringing the greatest gift of all, his story. This is a story for all of us, brimming with all good gifts.

*Questions to Ponder*

- How do you describe Christ's authority to others? What does the incarnation of Christ, the Christmas story, tell you about God's authority?
- Reflect upon what you might consider a weakness in yourself. How might God use this as a strength?

*Prayer*

God of all creation, in becoming weak you demonstrated the strength of your love and the gracious authority of your kingdom. Keep us this day, a day like no other, so that we might tell your humble and glorious story. Amen.

# Week 2: Renew Our Days

## *Day 8: Sunday*

### Daily Transformations
2 Corinthians 4:16-18; Psalm 16

> *Key Verse:* So we do not lose heart. Even though our outer nature
> is wasting away, our inner nature is being renewed day by day.
> 2 Corinthians 4:16

The very same day seen through different perspectives can seem bad or good, a burden or a blessing. For instance, if you look at all the interruptions, the petty annoyances and distractions that kept you from accomplishing all the tasks on your "to-do list" on a certain workday, you might end the day with great frustration. A sharp word from a colleague left a bitter taste after lunch, while you wondered what you might have done to deserve that remark. Family members surprised you with dinner after work, but rather than a pleasant surprise, all you noticed was the kitchen full of handprints, footprints, and flour dust they left behind. Your irritation only increased and your mood only grew worse, despite their obvious intentions to be helpful.

Perception does become our reality. Our translation of the meaning of events often determines our attitude by the end of the day. Maybe the petty annoyances gave you an opportunity to add more "people time" into your day. Perhaps the distractions reminded you that relationships are sometimes more important than tasks. That colleague's bitter comment might prompt you to wonder about her life. Could you offer a word of compassion, for Jesus' sake? And the mess in the kitchen—did you notice the pride on your daughter's face as she carried in the best macaroni and cheese in the whole world? Will this be another "remember when" moment in years to come, when she's grown and gone, with children of her own perhaps?

Sometimes we need to take a second look. God's Holy Spirit has a way of whispering quietly in the most unlikely times and places. Is there another way to look at this event or that moment? What difference would it make if you were seeing things, say, through God's eyes? How would you see your day? Your family? Yourself? As we look at the little things in life, we might glimpse God's healing at work to mend a broken heart, a shattered dream, or a ruptured relationship. Advent is a time to pray for the Holy Spirit to renew our perspective, deepen our wisdom, and help us watch for the unexpected ways, times, and places God comes to us and changes us from the inside out. Come, Lord Jesus.

## Questions to Ponder

- How might this season be a time of renewing your perspective and your faith?
- Think about a painful memory that needs God's healing or a new perspective. Consider how this pain in your past might allow you to give wisdom or comfort to someone else now.

## Prayer

Heavenly God, give us eyes to see and ears to hear your healing, redeeming presence in our lives today and always. Renew our perspective and help us celebrate the many gifts in our lives. Amen.

## Day 9: Monday

### Daily Encouragement

Isaiah 7:10-17; John 21:1-12

*Key Verse:* Just after daybreak, Jesus stood on the beach; but the disciples did not know that it was Jesus. John 21:4

Despite the eclectic mix and crazy jumble of Santa Claus, Baby Jesus, and Christmas lists, there are ways to be encouraged by the sights and sounds of this pre-Christmas season. It's encouraging to see so many public displays of Christian symbols in places where usually there are no clues that God might be present, real, and powerful. Sure, it's quirky—reindeer with moving heads poised just under a star that changes color, while an inflatable Mary and Joseph complete the lawn art at my neighbor's house. I have a pretty little angel that plays "Deck the Halls" and a Santa that "ho-ho's" so hard he falls off the mantel. But still. In this inelegant overload of mixed metaphors and tasteless icons, it's hard to go anywhere without being reminded that Christmas is coming.

With practice, we can search through the clutter and noise and select where and how to be reminded that God came, God comes, and God is still with us. We could let the overload of Christmas trinkets remind us that we can still celebrate our faith publicly—a freedom some countries don't grant their residents. Maybe this makes it easier to talk about faith publicly too. With some imagination (and maybe even practice) there are ways to slip in a little "witness" here and there, even as we stand in line to pay for gifts.

What if we tried on new, encouraging responses to the complaints we hear at this time of year? If someone says, "I'll be glad when it's over," try responding, "Yes, it's tiring, but everywhere you go there are 'God things' if you notice them. I always try to think, 'There's another reminder that God loves us.'" Or maybe you're in an elevator with loud, not particularly pleasant Christmas music, and someone complains, "That tinny music is so annoying!" You might say, "Yeah, it sounds a lot better on our church organ or when the congregation sings it." (That might just break the unspoken rule that we never mention our church practices in public!) And there are always those who grumble about shopping and spending too much. Wouldn't it be great to respond with, "Yeah, and all they really want to know is that we love them." Be brave—sometimes it just takes a few words to give someone a boost of encouragement. Share a word or two of faith, pure love in humble wrappings. God shows up in unexpected times and places—in conversations at the store, in a hospital elevator, in a barn out back in Bethlehem. That's the wonder of the season!

## Questions to Ponder

- In our commercial Christmas landscape, what can still encourage us that Jesus came to save the world and not condemn it?
- How might you encourage others to find hope and meaning in what so easily becomes the chaos of Christmas? Be creative!

## Prayer

Dear Lord, we treasure the gift that other believers are to us. Make us gifts to others. Help us to share the flame of your love and brighten the path for someone who is looking for light today. Amen.

## Day 10: Tuesday

### Daily Hunger

Matthew 4:3-4; Matthew 6:11; John 6:35; Isaiah 55:1-3

> *Key Verse:* But he answered, "It is written, 'One does not live by bread alone, but by every word that comes from the mouth of God.'" Matthew 4:4

We want so much to say "I love you" with the Christmas gifts we buy. And we've taught ourselves so well to expect excess that we feel somehow inadequate without it. So we eat, spend, and do too much. Then, when it's over, we diet, exchange our gifts, and feel guilty about credit card debt. We confess that we are in bondage and can't seem to free ourselves.

Could it be that the driving force behind the seductive lure of commercial Christmas excess is really just our age-old enemy at work once again? The devil told Jesus in the wilderness, "Command these stones to become loaves of bread." In other words, use your power just for yourself and your own needs. One of the deceiver's tricks is to encourage us to do a good thing at the wrong time. When Jesus was in the wilderness strengthening his self-control and ability to stay focused on God, it was the wrong time to focus on his own appetite. Here we are in a time to let gratitude and love spill over to the people in our lives, a spiritual season intended to help us meditate on ways to bring more peace and light into the world. How do we get trapped into a routine that often fuels greed instead of gratitude and a pace that cancels out contemplation? "No room, no room," the innkeepers said. "No time, no time," we so often say. And our old enemy smiles and says, "No God, no peace." "Go ahead and focus on filling your storehouses." He might add, "God won't mind, really."

Excess, junk food, and insatiable appetite—all these can be symptoms of spiritual malnutrition, a malnutrition that comes from practicing "Christianity a la carte," going to the dessert table first and picking up too much fluff and not enough protein. An unhealthy diet of too much, too fast, and too many shortcuts makes it difficult to enjoy the peace and blessings of faith in God. But Jesus said,

"I am the bread of life. Whoever comes to me will never be hungry, and whoever believes in me will never be thirsty" (John 6:35).

## Questions to Ponder

- When have you been the most content about the balance in your life? When have you felt balanced about the way you keep Christmas?
- If you are caught in the cycle of "too much, too fast, and too many short-cuts," where might you begin to break free?

## Prayer

Dear Jesus, release us from filling our lives with things that do not satisfy our hunger. Help us turn to you for daily bread. Where we have too much, teach us to share with those who are less fortunate. Amen.

# Day 11: Wednesday

## Daily Purpose

Ephesians 2:8-10; Mark 12:28-31

> *Key Verse:* For we are what he has made us, created in Christ Jesus
> for good works, which God prepared beforehand to be our way of
> life. Ephesians 2:10

Images of "the good life" bombard us day after day in every form of advertising. How does this relate to the way of life God imagines for us? What does a well-lived Christian life look like? Is it more than being kind when we can and generous as we are able?

Without a sense of purpose or meaning, we spend our lives running around in circles.

We chase after "the good life" and search for our own happiness or success. Jesus calls us to give up that way of life, along with the little kingdoms we try to create for ourselves. He calls us to a greater purpose, a broader vision, a noble and excellent pursuit: the way of service and following him.

The greatest commandment, Jesus said, is to love God and to love our neighbors as ourselves. The trouble is that we often misunderstand the word *love*. Love is an action, a way of life, a doing, not a thought or a feeling. This doing happens as we join with other believers and carry out God's work in the world.

Love as a way of life means no more running around in circles for us as individuals and faith communities. If we are actively engaged in helping others, that affects our priorities for each day. It changes what we put on our calendars, how we think about success, and where we put our passion and resources. It's been said that where your resources and the world's needs meet, there you'll find God's purpose for your life. People who are the most content with life see meaning in their daily living and have a sense of belonging in a group or community. Following Jesus and serving him in the world gives congregations a clear sense of purpose and a clear connection among the people.

God created us with a purpose in mind. When we follow "the way, and the truth, and the life" (John 14:6), we do so much more than run around in circles and find so much more satisfaction in our living. In carrying out God's purpose, we live out the abundant life (John 10:10) that Jesus came to bring us.

*Questions to Ponder*

- What resources has God given you? Which needs in the world could be served with these resources?
- If you handed your activity calendar or checkbook to a friend, would your Christian faith show up among your priorities?

*Prayer*

God of love, remind me today why I'm here and show me where I can serve and bless others. Help me bring your light to someone's darkness today. Amen.

# Day 12: Thursday

## Daily Integrity and Peace
Matthew 6:25-34; 7:7-8; Luke 2:13-14; Isaiah 59:8

🔲 *Key Verse:* But strive first for the kingdom of God and his righteousness, and all these things will be given to you as well. Matthew 6:33

Peace with God doesn't make sense unless we understand and experience how often our desires don't match up with God's preferred values. What keeps you awake on those nights you can't sleep? What eats at your soul when you feel like you're fighting a current without a paddle? Why does unresolved conflict and anger at others cause us so much inner turmoil? The warfare in our souls, the tug that pulls us back and forth between me first and God first, can make all of life feel like a struggle. Sometimes this struggle isn't even conscious; we just carry the battle scars in our bodies.

The truth is that the anxiety that has become so much a part of our way of life is often caused by confusion about what we really value, believe, or can com- mit our hearts to. We are afraid of missing out, because we want it all. We don't have a well-developed value system that we trust to guide us. So our choices about time are shaped by a consumer mentality: what's in it for me?

Without the ability to make commitments, we are constantly tossed to and fro in a sea of choices that never lets us rest. How can we possibly be at peace with God, ourselves, or our neighbors if we feel lost at sea, with nothing but impulse and appetite to guide us? Deep down we know there are wiser guide- lines for living. Could it be that the surrender and obedience the Bible talks about are ways out of our restlessness? Could service to others actually bring us some peace? And all the talk of spiritual depth and maturity and the pres- ence of God, is that real? What demons do we have to wrestle with before God can break through? Perhaps we will never know until we really *stop*. Instead of saying, "Don't just sit there, do something," maybe it's time to say, "Don't just do something, sit there."

A relationship with God, like any relationship, takes time. It changes who we are and how we think. And before the old really passes away—because we keep grabbing it back when we're uncomfortable—we need to stop *thinking about God* and start *talking with God*. God's love is pure gift, but you have to sit down and unwrap it. Ponder it, examine it, respond to it, and integrate it into your identity. In all your ways acknowledge God, and you will be on the path that leads to peace, integrity, and rest for your soul.

## Questions to Ponder

- Pause throughout this day and ask God to carry whatever is bothering you and to give you peace. What difference does this make in your day?
- At the end of the day, ask the Spirit to spread mercy and grace over any guilt from today and wisdom over your day tomorrow. Then rest in peace. Live knowing that God nurtures your faith and helps it to grow.

## Prayer

Dear Jesus, your perfect love casts out fear. Renew our relationships with God, ourselves, and our neighbors. Help us listen for your messages of peace. Amen.

# Day 13: Friday

## Daily Compassion

Isaiah 58:5-9

> 💬 *Key Verse:* Is not this the fast that I choose: to loose the bonds of injustice, to undo the thongs of the yoke, to let the oppressed go free, and to break every yoke? Isaiah 58:6

How can there be a God when there's so much suffering in the world? How can Christianity be a good thing when so much evil has been done in the name of the church? You've probably heard someone ask these questions, or asked them yourself. And maybe you've heard this too: "Christians are such hypocrites. They are always fighting over the silliest things."

In a turbulent world where millions of people go to bed hungry, homeless, and persecuted by unjust laws and governments, what are we waiting for? Why aren't we getting more involved? Why aren't we doing more to fight hunger, homelessness, and injustice? If we take what the Bible says as important, we can hardly ignore the lifestyle we are called to live. It's much easier to find excuses not to be involved in God's work and God's world, but if we want God to do something about suffering, we need to stand ready to be part of the answer to our prayers. You see, we are God's hands and feet in the world.

The story of the rich man and Lazarus (Luke 16:19-31) is a hard one for most of us to hear. The rich man walked by and never noticed the street person, Lazarus, sitting at the gate and asking for water. People like Lazarus are the very people Jesus points us to: those who are poor, those who are homeless, those who are grieving, those without families—the very people we might ignore and pass by on a busy sidewalk. Would we welcome a homeless person into our congregation? Would a widow or orphan without clean clothes be invited to enjoy a potluck meal with us?

What is God calling us to be and to do in all of this? Look at how God reaches those in need. The touch of God's grace moves followers of Christ from minding our own business and helplessly accepting the world's brokenness to active involvement and reaching out to our neighbors. Listen to the stories of people who travel and go on mission trips to serve people living in poverty. Check out how congregations allow us to work together to help those in need. In those times when we respond with compassion and really make a difference in the lives of others, faith is nourished and we are involved in God's work of making all things new. The baby who comes so quietly is still motivating us to respond with compassion, to be blessings to others, and to be God's hands and feet in the world.

*Questions to Ponder*

- When was the last time you went out of your way to bless a stranger or acquaintance when they didn't expect it?
- What are some of the ways you feel blessed to serve?

*Prayer*

God of compassion, thank you for giving us opportunities to serve others. Thank you for sending your Holy Spirit to gather us together in such a way that we really can make a difference to people we could never reach on our own. Open our eyes this season to places where people deeply need your touch. Amen.

# Day 14: Saturday

## Daily Focus

Philippians 4:8-19

> 📱 *Key Verse:* Finally, beloved, whatever is true, whatever is honorable, whatever is just, whatever is pure, whatever is pleasing, whatever is commendable, if there is any excellence and if there is anything worthy of praise, think about these things. Philippians 4:8

Sometimes our inner thoughts and feelings run amok and seem entirely out of control, or at least like they have lives of their own. Yet psychologists emphasize that what we focus on is often a choice, even though it may not always feel like a choice. Focusing on love is a choice. Focusing on fear is a choice. And focusing on joy is a choice. Some call this "threshold thinking"—don't let self-destructive, unworthy, bitter, or dark thoughts cross into the habits of your mind. Stop them before they take up energy and residence in your daily life. "Just don't go there," my kids might say. "It's not worth the trip."

The prayer used by Alcoholics Anonymous groups puts it well: "God, grant me the serenity to accept the things I cannot change, courage to change the things I can, and the wisdom to know the difference." In his letter to the Philippians, the apostle Paul simply says, in essence, focus on the good. Is this merely an escape technique that allows us to ignore the brokenness in ourselves and others? Consider what happens when we spend time fueling our fears. As we get lost in all the bad news in the world, we become more and more fearful and mistrustful of everyone else. Sometimes we lose hope and any motivation to work at making things better.

Maybe this is why Scripture has a lot to say about what we focus on. If you want to focus on finding fault, focus on your own shortcomings. Start with the log in your own eye. If you want more material goods than you have, consider the lilies of the field in all their glory, or the children on the street who go to bed hungry. If the world around you seems chaotic and full of darkness, shine God's light. Grieve, but not as someone who has no hope. Focus on God's goodness and not on the world's imperfections or your own. God makes promises and keeps them. You are God's beloved child. God hears and answers your prayers. God is with us at all times, even when we are facing death.

Paul, who endured suffering, shipwrecks, and imprisonment, said we would be amazed at how content we can be in any circumstances. Whether in situations of plenty or of want, he focused on Christ his Lord and rejoiced in him. God cares for us and pours out blessings on us every day. On top of this, we have the joy of sharing God's love and blessings with others. Joy—daily and lasting joy—is a gift from God for all the world.

## Questions to Ponder

- What's the difference between happiness and joy? When have you truly experienced joy?
- What does it tell us about God that the joy of Christ's birth is for all the world? How will the world know about this?

## Prayer

Faithful God, thank you for giving us eternal hope through Jesus that makes daily joy possible. Renew our hope and joy this season, and help us tell it on the mountains and in the valleys of our days. Amen.

# Week 3: Renew Our Spirits

## *Day 15: Sunday*

### Total Renewal of Spirit

John 3:1-16

*Key Verse:* Very truly, I tell you, no one can see the kingdom of God without being born from above. John 3:3

In this Advent season, we think *new*—a new church year, a new baby born at Christmas. Today the Bible reading calls us to think of ourselves as new—the complete renewal of our spirits, our very selves, by God's gracious work. Real renewal is totally new existence through God's Spirit. Like this one, many Bible passages promise renewal of our spirits. Always this renewal is the work of God, not our own work. Our spirits are entirely dependent on God for new existence.

In John 3, Jesus tells Nicodemus, a Jewish leader, that no one can see the kingdom of God without being born of water and the Spirit. This rebirth, or renewal, comes "from above." Nicodemus misunderstands the point Jesus is making. He hears Jesus saying that we must be born "again," which is also a meaning of the Greek word. Jesus is speaking not of a second physical birth, however, but of a new birth from above. God's Holy Spirit gives true renewal and makes our spirits alive. This renewal is total rebirth of the person, a new existence through God's Spirit. Only God can make such new birth possible. Through the work of God in Christ, we become a new being. This eternal heavenly life comes only through the Son of God (John 3:16). The Spirit enables us to know and believe in Jesus, and so have eternal life (John 3:15, 36). What an incredible gift of renewal! All other renewal in our lives flows from this renewal.

I come from Australia, where a large part of the continent is desert. It's the driest permanently inhabited continent on earth, exceeded only by Antarctica.

The earth is dry, yellow-beige or rust-red, with only occasional tufts of yellow-beige spiky grass, as far as the eye can see. Dry. All very dead. But every few years an amazing transformation takes place. Rain sweeps across the land. The desert suddenly explodes into new life—plants and flowers spring up. Insects swarm. Spiders, reptiles, mice, and other animals breed. Just for a short while, there is beauty and fertility. But the new life is transient; the rain ceases and soon all is dry and dead again.

We are dead, dry, perishable creatures. But God takes our dead, sinful, dry persons and makes them new, alive, children of the Holy One. Unlike the desert rain, this gift of renewal is eternal. Daily, the Holy Spirit pours overflowing life into us. Through our baptism we are born of water and the Spirit (John 3:5). God gives us forgiveness and new being by grace through faith. God's Spirit makes and keeps us alive, not just for this world but for the world to come with Christ.

## Questions to Ponder

- Do you really want total renewal? What kinds of commitment might God ask of you?
- How will baptism affect your life this day? Tomorrow? If you have any reminders of your baptism (certificate, candle, photos), get them out and look at them. Or reflect on a baptism you have witnessed.

## Prayer

O God, thank you for the gift of eternal life. Give us today that renewal of spirit that only you can give by the power of your Spirit. Birth us from above, forgive our sin, and live in us to serve and do your will, through Jesus Christ our Lord. Amen.

# Day 16: Monday

## Renewal of Spirit through Relationship

Romans 8:1-17

> *Key Verse:* For you did not receive a spirit of slavery to fall back into fear, but you have received a spirit of adoption. When we cry, "Abba! Father!" it is that very Spirit bearing witness with our spirit that we are children of God. Romans 8:15-16

What an amazing set of promises and good news we have in Romans 8:1-17! God gives us renewal of our spirits through establishing a new relationship with us in Jesus Christ. We are adopted as God's children.

Paul begins Romans 8 by telling us that those who are in Christ Jesus are no longer condemned. Even though we deserve judgment because of sin, our sin is forgiven freely through Christ Jesus, who once and for all has fulfilled the law on our behalf, and thus sets us free from the law of sin and death. So now our lives are new. We walk according to the Spirit, and the Spirit sets us free and gives us liberty, life, and peace. The powerful Holy Spirit, who raised Jesus from the dead, now lives in us. The Spirit has set us into a new relationship with God, created when Christ went to the cross. The Spirit gives us faith—faith to believe that Christ's death was for us and for our forgiveness. So we are daily led by the Spirit as children of God.

The Holy Spirit bears witness with our spirit that we are indeed God's adopted children. As adopted members of God's family, we truly call God "Papa" (Abba) and "Father." We dare to address God as a loved child addresses a dear parent. As God's very own offspring, we are heirs of God and co-inheritors with Christ. In this world we suffer with Christ; in the next we share Christ's glory. By the Holy Spirit of God, our spirits are conformed to the crucified Christ.

Adoption makes it clear that God has chosen to be gracious to us. We are made God's own in spite of sin. Forgiveness is the basis of renewal of our spirits. Our renewal is not our own doing, nor is it something we deserve—it is a matter of grace and pure gift from God.

This good news has transformed countless lives. Martin Luther spent years as a monk seeking to earn God's approval. The gospel of free forgiveness of sin through Christ changed Luther from self-flagellating monk to proclaimer of God's grace and leader of the Reformation, which was centered on justification by grace through faith.

John Henry Newton was a sailor who worked in the slave trade. He experienced a spiritual conversion while at sea, and later left the slave trade and trained for priesthood in the Church of England. An ally of William Wilberforce, Newton worked for the abolition of slavery. He wrote some of the most beloved hymns that celebrate God's grace and love—among them "Amazing grace, how sweet the sound" and "How sweet the name of Jesus sounds."

*Amazing grace!—how sweet the sound—that saved a wretch like me! I once was lost, but now am found; was blind, but now I see.* (ELW 779)

## Questions to Ponder

- What does God's free forgiveness mean to you?
- How does being an adopted child of God change your life and make you new?

## Prayer

Abba, Father, thank you for the inestimable privilege of being called your adopted children. Help us to rejoice in this relationship and to experience it in prayer daily, through Christ our Lord. Amen.

## Day 17: Tuesday

### God's Promise of a New Spirit

Ezekiel 11:14-21; 37:1-14

> 💬 *Key Verse:* I will give them one heart, and put a new spirit within
> them; I will remove the heart of stone from their flesh and give them
> a heart of flesh, so that they may follow my statutes and keep my
> ordinances and obey them. Then they shall be my people, and I will
> be their God. Ezekiel 11:19-20

The year 597 B.C.E. was a dark one in the life of Israel. The Babylonians carried a number of the people into exile, including the priest Ezekiel. Even worse, the deportation was followed in 586 B.C.E. by yet another large contingent being exiled to Babylon. In this foreign land, Ezekiel was called by God to be a prophet to the exiles. Ezekiel told of God's judgments on Israel, but also of hope for a new age to come. He had great faith in the unmerited grace of God.

In Ezekiel 11 we read of God's gracious promise to put a new spirit within the people of Israel. The chapter starts with denunciations but then turns to a promise of future restoration. The LORD will gather the scattered people and bring them home and restore the land to them. Through pure grace, God will give the people a new heart and put a new spirit within them, transforming their stony hearts into soft hearts of flesh. Inwardly renewed, the people will obey and serve God and once more be children of the covenant.

A later vision, in Ezekiel 37:1-14, provides a wonderful image of the renewal of the people of God. Read it through and picture the scene in your mind. Ezekiel stands in the middle of a valley full of dry bones. All vitality has long since gone from these bones. Starkly dead, indeed. God asks, "Mortal, can these bones live?" Ezekiel answers, "O Lord GOD, you know!" And God does know! So God tells Ezekiel to prophesy to the bones, and the prophet tells the bones that God will restore them to life. There is a rattling, and the bones come together. Then sinews attach to the bones. Flesh and skin cover them. But there is no life, not yet. Then the breath of the Lord GOD breathes upon the bodies, and they live once more—a vast living multitude renewed and on their feet! Israel's hope had been lost in the exile. The people feel as dead as those bones in the valley. But as Ezekiel is told to prophesy to his people, God will revive the despairing exiles and bring them back to the land of Israel.

Sometimes we are dead as dry bones. When faith and hope seem lost, when we despair, we can turn to God. God's Spirit breathes on us when we feel there is no life left in us. God gives us a new spirit and revives us when we ourselves feel hopeless and unable to help ourselves. God brings us into a good place where we recognize God's renewing work in our lives. God brings hope and restores faith. Yes, we can thank God for renewal of spirit through mercy and grace and power given from the one who is Life itself.

### Questions to Ponder

- Think of a time when your heart was stony. How did God change it?
- How does the story of Ezekiel speak to you of God's unfailing love and power to renew us and give us a new spirit?

### Prayer

O God, transform our stony hearts into soft hearts of faith and obedience to you. Give us a new spirit as you promised through the prophet Ezekiel. When we are dead as dry bones, breathe your Spirit into us and revive us to live and love and serve you daily, in the name of Jesus. Amen.

## Day 18: Wednesday

### Renewal of Mind

Romans 12:1-13

> *Key Verse:* Do not be conformed to this world, but be transformed by the renewing of your minds, so that you may discern what is the will of God—what is good and acceptable and perfect. Romans 12:2

One way God renews our spirits is by renewing our minds. You have probably heard the saying "A mind is a terrible thing to waste." God doesn't just prevent our minds from wasting. God renews our minds! God transforms our minds so that we may hear and understand God's will and promises.

When Paul talks about renewal of our minds, he is thinking of a radical transformation at the core of our personality. The response to God's saving work is to offer all our faculties to God for complete transformation—by God, not by ourselves. God will transform our whole selves, all that we are. We are given a revolution in our thinking, a new sensitivity to what life in the new age looks like.

The renewal of our minds and our spirits is the work of God the Holy Spirit, who shows us that the shape of the life of faith is humility (Romans 12:3) and love (12:9-10). The life of faith is ardent, rejoicing, patient, persevering, prayerful, generous, and hospitable (12:11-13). God gives us different gifts that together build up the body of Christ (12:4-8). These gifts come from Christ, and we are called to use them for building up the church. Pride, boasting, and division have no place in the body of Christ, the assembly of believers who live in the new age and gather around Word and sacraments for the forgiveness of sin.

A renewed mind returns daily to the gospel. Because our minds, like the rest of us, are tainted by sin, they need repeated cleansing and forgiveness. A renewed mind turns to the Scriptures and seeks God's guidance to read them aright and to hear the word of rebuke and the word of mercy and salvation in the biblical text. A renewed mind prays that God will help us understand and remember the great deeds that God has done.

Paul knew all about transformation of mind and personality. On the road to Damascus, Christ encountered Saul. Christ changed Saul from a persecutor, breathing threats and murder against the Lord's disciples, into the great apostle Paul, who would establish churches throughout the Mediterranean region. God used Paul's great intellect by having Paul write letters and serve as the primary theologian of the early church. God used Paul's heart to love and care for the fledgling congregations, even when they tried his patience to the uttermost. God gave Paul faith to continue his missionary work despite imprisonment, stoning, shipwreck, hunger, thirst, and other dangers. What a change of personality and mind! Paul considered himself "unfit to be called an apostle" because of his persecution of the church. But the grace of God made him the missionary apostle he came to be (1 Corinthians 15:9-10). We read his letters today to hear the heart of the good news of Jesus Christ for us and for our salvation.

## Questions to Ponder

·    How does God use your mind?
·    How does the Spirit help you daily to hear God's Word in the Scriptures? What rebuke or promise do you hear in the Scripture passage today?

## Prayer

Take our minds and renew them, O God. Teach us to think in ways that flow from your renewal of our spirits. Help us to understand more of your great works and learn to express the gospel in ways that others can understand and believe, for Christ's sake. Amen.

## Day 19: Thursday

### Renewal of Strength

Isaiah 40:12-31

> 💬 *Key Verse:* Those who wait for the LORD shall renew their strength, they shall mount up with wings like eagles, they shall run and not be weary, they shall walk and not faint. Isaiah 40:31

Today's Bible passage is part of a prophecy to a weary and despondent nation exiled in Babylon. The poet-prophet announces that God's salvation for the exiles is just around the corner. God will come with mighty deliverance. Only the Creator of the world can bring about the seemingly impossible—the deliverance of the people. The nations are as nothing before the Lord of history, the everlasting God, the Creator of the ends of the earth. This great God gives power to the faint. What comfort for a weary and powerless people! Those who wait for the Lord—those who wait expectantly for the fulfillment of God's promises and for salvation—will have their strength renewed. They shall rise up like eagles, run and not become tired, walk and not faint. God is the source of their renewal and vigor.

This passage also is a word of comfort to us today. God renews our spirits by renewing our strength. Have you ever felt weak? Powerless? Despairing? Have you ever felt that you cannot go on for one more day? God promises to comfort us and renew our strength. We wait on the Lord—we look expectantly to God, who will do great things for us according to God's promises.

Have you ever watched an eagle take flight, soaring on powerful wings high in the sky? Have you watched marathon runners pounding rhythmically for miles, seemingly with little effort? Maybe you have seen walkers who cover four or five miles a day on a track or on your neighborhood streets, without too much huffing and puffing. Perhaps we look enviously at those who run and seem not to get tired. Some of us have more strength than others when it comes to physical activity.

But it is the hardships of life that really test us—the loneliness and weariness of life, the exiles of our own making, the pressure of daily existence in the modern world, the inability to plod on, let alone run or fly, in our daily lives. But God promises to renew our strength so that we can go on and endure, whatever the situation we must face. By grace we can soar on eagles' wings, can run without becoming weary, can stride on without collapsing.

How easy it is to forget God and God's promises in this Advent season. There is so much to do! We busy ourselves with shopping, cooking, gift wrapping, card writing, decorating, pageants, visiting, and a whole lot more. Prayer is often the last thing on our minds. We need to pause during this season to tell God in what ways we feel weak and helpless and to pray for renewed strength to be God's servants in the world.

## Questions to Ponder

- For what do you need strength today? This week?
- In what ways has God strengthened you in the past? How can memories of God's work in your life give you courage to face what might be around the bend?

## Prayer

O God, our strength and comfort, give us renewal that we might face the future with zeal and with faith. Help us to soar like eagles, run like marathoners, walk purposefully and surely through life, in the knowledge that you are the one on whom we can depend, in Christ's name. Amen.

## Day 20: Friday

### Renewed Spirit for Mission

Acts 2:1-21, 29-36

*Key Verse:* Therefore let the entire house of Israel know with certainty that God has made him both Lord and Messiah, this Jesus whom you crucified. Acts 2:36

The stranger on the subway was grading papers. I asked how he enjoyed teaching. "Do you know why I teach?" he asked. I shook my head. "It is because I believe that God has been very good to me and has given me gifts for teaching. So I want to thank God and use my gifts to help others. That is why I teach," he said. Then he went on to discuss various aspects of teaching that he enjoyed. His witness was natural, not at all forced. A simple and true answer to my question. I was glad I had asked. This man had gifts for witnessing. It was simply a part of his life. I was impressed. How many of us would speak so naturally about our faith to a complete stranger?

God renews our spirits for mission. If we care to listen, God will show us the occasions in which we can speak a word for God and the church. But sometimes we are afraid to speak about God. We wonder if our words will offend. We remember that some people think religion is a purely private affair. Our mouths remain shut, and we turn to look out the window rather than strike up a conversation.

After Jesus' resurrection, his disciples are afraid. If they speak about Jesus, they might be arrested. They huddle together behind closed doors. After Jesus' ascension, they obey Jesus' order to wait in Jerusalem for God's promise. When the day of Pentecost arrives, they are together. Then God acts with power they have never before experienced. The God who descended to Mount Sinai in fire (Exodus 19:18) now descends in flames of the Spirit. The Spirit fills the disciples, and they are renewed—no longer a fearful, cowering group huddling together for strength, but a fiery group of witnesses marching out into the public square. And Peter preaches a sermon the likes of which the crowds have never heard. He witnesses to Jesus, crucified and risen. "God has made him both Lord and

Messiah, this Jesus whom you crucified." Cut to the heart, three thousand become believers and are baptized.

The day of Pentecost demonstrates the power of the Spirit's renewal for mission—a group of frightened disciples are turned into a living witness that draws huge numbers to faith. God can do that for us too!

At Pentecost the Spirit filled all of the disciples—*all* of them, even though some may have had more ability than others, some may have been more likeable, some may have spoken more eloquently. All were recipients of the Spirit's power and gifts. No one was excluded. We may not think that we can be witnesses, but we can, because God can and will renew us for the purpose. Witnessing is not the work of pastors alone, or missionaries alone, or great church leaders alone. Witnessing is the work of everyone who names the name of Jesus Christ.

## Questions to Ponder

- If a stranger asked you why you go to church, what would you say?
- What wonderful things has God done for you that you want to share with others?

## Prayer

Spirit of God, you gave gifts and strength to the disciples on the day of Pentecost. Give us a longing to share the good news with others, and teach us how to speak naturally and honestly of your love and forgiveness, in Jesus' name. Amen.

## Day 21: Saturday

## Prayer for a New Spirit

Psalm 51:1-17

> 💬 *Key Verse:* Create in me a clean heart, O God, and put a new and right spirit within me. Psalm 51:10

Advent is a time for prayer. What better time to pray for God to put a new and right spirit within us.

The psalmist knows that the source of a new spirit is God alone. First, the penitent psalmist acknowledges his sin and asks for forgiveness: "Blot out my transgressions" (Psalm 51:1). That is the work of God, to forgive sin. Then the psalmist prays for a clean heart and a new and right spirit. Keep me in your presence, God! Restore to me the joy of your salvation. Sustain me and deliver me. Help me to praise you.

The psalmist knows full well that it is because of God's mercy that we can come to God in repentance and pray for forgiveness. As Christians, we know that God's mercy was shown primarily in Christ. The gracious work of God in Christ precedes our prayers. It already stands for us, and did so even before we were born. That's what baptism is all about. God loved us and died for us before we even knew anything about it. Now that's grace! God is willing to forgive us in spite of our sinfulness, just because that is what God is like. And forgiveness of sin is necessary for the restoration of a relationship with God, who is our Savior.

By our own efforts we cannot create in ourselves a clean heart or a new spirit. So, like the psalmist, we pray for God to put a new and right spirit within us. This new spirit is not just a once-and-never-again gift. God can make our spirit new every day. So we turn to God in prayer daily. And we return to our baptism daily. That means we remember that in our baptism we died and rose with Christ for the forgiveness of sin. Every day we need that washing. Every day we need to hear the gospel. And we can believe it, be certain of it, because Christ was crucified for us before we ever knew about it. Martin Luther found it comforting to remind himself, "I am baptized." We can find comfort in remembering our baptism also.

In this time of Advent we prepare for Christmas. We will soon be praising God for the incarnation of the Son of God for our salvation. We are dependent on God for the ability to pray and to praise God aright. This is a great time to kneel at the manger and ask for God to give us a clean heart and a new and right spirit, so that we truly can offer God adoration, repentance, love, and thanksgiving for Christ.

## Questions to Ponder

- How does Psalm 51 help us to confess to God? Why do you think we use it on Ash Wednesday and at other times of repentance and renewal?
- What other psalms help you to pray? You might turn to some of the following: Psalms 23; 119:89-112; 121; 138; 143; 145; 148; 150; and any other favorites.

## Prayer

We turn to you, O God, asking for forgiveness and renewal. Give us clean hearts and put a new and right spirit within us. Help us in this Advent season to put you in the center of our lives and thoughts as we prepare to celebrate the coming of your Son, in whose name we pray. Amen.

# Week 4: Renew Our Ways

## Day 22: Sunday

### Discovering Someplace New

Mark 6:1-6

> *Key Verse:* Is not this the carpenter, the son of Mary and brother of James and Joses and Judas and Simon, and are not his sisters here with us? Mark 6:3

Christopher Columbus has gone down in history as a great explorer. This he was, though a huge ego and an often difficult personality dull many of his achievements. So does the cruelty he inflicted on whole tribes of indigenous people in the Caribbean. By all accounts he died a bitter man, nursing his grievances against the king of Spain and a host of other individuals he believed had cheated him of wealth.

Elizabeth Kolbert summarizes the tragedy of Columbus's life as his reluctance to acknowledge the magnitude of what he had discovered. His stubbornness kept him insisting that Cuba was really part of China and that he had found the gateway to Asia. "In four trips across the ocean, he never . . . came upon anything remotely like what he had expected: not only were the people novel and strange; so were the geography, the topography, the flora, and the fauna. . . . He didn't want to have discovered someplace new; he wanted to have reached someplace old, and, as a result, was blind to the real nature of the world he had stumbled onto" ("The Lost Mariner," *The New Yorker*, October 14, 2002).

Limited vision is not only a matter of the eyes; it's also a crisis of narrow imagination. Sometimes we only see what we want to see. Columbus wasn't the first or the last person to revert to the comfort of his own assumptions. We all do it. We like our worldview to match up with our tastes and preferences. The major drawback to this myopic behavior is that we miss out on some wonderful realities right in front of our eyes. We shortchange a renewal of perspective in order to protect certain prejudices.

When Jesus came home to Nazareth after a period of travel, his old neighbors didn't know what to do with him. They mocked him for pretending to be someone he was not. They perceived him as something of a joke, even a fraud. His mighty deeds of power didn't match up with their expectations of him. How could this nondescript neighborhood kid grow up to be functioning like a divine wonder-worker? The two didn't go together.

The unwillingness of these hometown folks to see the glory of God at work through the words and actions of Jesus bothered him. He was amazed at their unbelieving ways. How would they ever see what they did not expect to find? When these neighbors would not pursue a more expansive vision of the world and of their lives, Jesus was no longer interested in working among them. He would move on.

### Questions to Ponder

- Onetime Harvard University president Charles Eliot once addressed the incoming freshman class with these words: "Don't tell me what you value. Tell me what you take for granted and never question." What are some of the things in your life that you take for granted and never question?
- Where does stubbornness get in the way of your availability to God?

### Prayer

Lord, your capacity to do amazing things right in front of our eyes is what we want to cherish today. Renew our vision for seeing things not as we wish they were, but as they really are. Amen.

## Day 23: Monday

### Time for a New Wardrobe

Ephesians 4:17-24

> 🔖 *Key Verse:* Clothe yourselves with the new self, created according to the likeness of God in true righteousness and holiness. Ephesians 4:24

What would it be like if wearing certain apparel actually changed something about our inner being? What if our character was surprisingly altered, or our hopes dramatically changed, just by dressing in different ways? This may actually be the private desire of some people. Throw on a jazzy sweater and others may view you as colorful. Dress in bright Bermuda plaid shorts on a summer day and acquaintances may suddenly think of you as carefree and fun.

Clothing communicates. It sends signals. There is little disagreement about this. The textiles and patterns with which we fill our closets and cover our bodies will always be connected with something personal about us, even if we aren't trying to make a statement. But can those same clothes really change us?

The British humorist Max Beerbohm wrote a delightful essay titled "The Happy Hypocrite" in 1897. In the story, the disgustingly self-centered main character is a man named Lord George Hell. He is a corrupt and degenerate soul, known for his overindulgence. His bloated and pockmarked face reveals his messed-up internal life.

Something happens to George one day. He falls in love with a beautiful woman and determines to marry her. Realizing the odds against him, given his ugly appearance, he dons the mask of a saint. He looks kind and now begins to behave virtuously. After some courting, he indeed succeeds in marrying the woman, and they live happily ever after.

One day, a woman from George's wicked past shows up and is not fooled. She knows that a wretched man's face is behind this mask, a face to match the scoundrel trying to hide. This woman confronts George in the presence of his wife. She challenges him to take off the mask, which he eventually does. Now the bloated and ugly face is gone. The face of the saint on the mask has become

George's own face. A magical transformation has made him the person of love that he had embodied while wearing the mask.

This is a mythical story, but an instructive one nonetheless. It gives insight into several passages of Paul in the New Testament, where the apostle speaks of the need for Christians to wear the right apparel. Paul was speaking metaphorically, not literally about the style of jeans to put on. But if we want to renew our lives every day and align our behaviors with the holiness of God, we need to put our dirty laundry in the hamper and dress in the baptismal grace that is ours. Every day!

## Questions to Ponder

- Think about a certain outfit you wear on special occasions. Why do you wear this particular outfit?
- Read Ephesians 4:17-32 and make a list of all the sins that apply to your personality and life. Think hard and truthfully about each one. Create a prayer referencing those maladies and your desire to be renewed by Christ.

## Prayer

Lord, sometimes we get attached to unhealthy behaviors, fudging the truth and living self-centered lives. Today, grant that all of this unclean laundry would end up in the hamper, so that we might dress instead in the robe of Christ's righteousness. Amen.

## Day 24: Tuesday

### Waking Up to a Brand-New Day

Lamentations 3:22-25

*Key Verse:* The steadfast love of the LORD never ceases, his mercies never come to an end; they are new every morning. Lamentations 3:22-23a

Christian people are at their best when they consider their lives as unfinished products. They remain open to renewal and growth. They get excited about becoming better people. This is not to say they aspire to become better than other people, just better than themselves.

Perhaps you have heard the line, or used the phrase: "This is just the way I am. I suggest you get used to it." We usually speak in such a manner when we're busy digging in our heels and unwilling to yield ground in a relationship. It is certainly not "becoming" speech. In fact, it sounds like we may have watched a little too much Popeye the Sailor Man. One of his favorite aphorisms was, "I yam what I yam and I yam what I yam that I yam. . . . That's the way it is 'til the day that I drop. . . . I yam what I yam."

In Christ, it is not good enough to merely say, "I am what I am . . . so tough for you!" No, every day brings new possibilities. The Scriptures tell us that the mercies of God are new every morning. The resentments and missteps of yesterday do not have to walk with us today. In fact, they have no right to accompany us today! God has rolled over the calendar page and given birth to a new sunrise precisely so that we might get a sense of what it means to be reborn.

When the great Spanish cellist Pablo Casals was in the later years of his life, he spoke to an interviewer about his daily ritual. "Each day I am reborn. Each day I must begin again. For the past 80 years I have started each day in the same manner. . . . I go to the piano and I play two preludes of Bach . . . it is a benediction on the house. But that is not its only meaning for me." Lest this holy observance sounds even remotely monotonous, Casals explains: "It is a rediscovery of the world of which I have the joy of being a part. It fills me with the wonder of eternity, with the incredible miracle of God. The music is never the same for me. Each day it is something new, fantastic, and unbelievable."

Wow. Imagine having this joyous approach to every new day. The good news of Jesus Christ comes alive for us whenever we say, "Today, I *must* begin again." One of the surprises of God is the grace we are given to surround this *must* with meaningful rituals that behold the holiness of life.

## Questions to Ponder

- Outline your own patterns for beginning a typical day. What are you proud of, and what could afford some reconsideration?
- Make some kind of journal entry that describes different ways that you show mercy or receive mercy. (Look up *mercy* in a dictionary if you need to get your juices flowing.)

## Prayer

O Gracious God, who seems unwilling to let your flow of loving-kindness stop or your inclination to be merciful cease, grant us a fresh capacity to see the newness of each day. Help us behold all that is fantastic and unbelievable about this particular day. Amen.

## Day 25: Wednesday

### Giving Birth

Isaiah 66:7-11

🔹 *Key Verse:* Shall a land be born in one day? Shall a nation be delivered in one moment? Isaiah 66:8b

I have a friend whose wife was pregnant with their first child. At the outset, Matt was more nervous than excited. He was anxious about the financial implications of adding a child to their lives, and he was unsure that he would adequately fill the responsibilities that go with being a good parent. One day he decided to put his nervous energies into a big project—building a crib from scratch. In short order, the pencil sketch became a wood order, and everything was under way. He headed out to his woodworking shop in the garage nearly every day after work, hoping to make headway.

Weeks of sawing, planing, gluing, and staining turned into months. It's a good thing the gestation period for humans is nine months. Matt needed most of that time to finish. An interesting thing happened along the way, however. He got more and more excited about this coming baby, and less and less nervous. Time alone in the wood shop functioned like an exercise in renewal. Slowly but surely, he was coming to terms with the new person this birth required him to be.

During Advent, it's a good idea to read from biblical passages like Isaiah 66. The rich maternal imagery used for God in these sections is a healthy contrast to the often masculine and muscular theology spoken in church circles. God is about to give birth, and we have only four weeks—not thirty-eight weeks—to prepare ourselves.

It may seem a silly thing to talk about preparing ourselves for a divine pregnancy. But preparation is a spiritual requirement for every meaningful birth. Meister Eckhart, the thirteenth-century mystic, put it in a memorable way, using words that still ring true for our own Advent journey:

We are all meant to be mothers of God. What good is it to me if this eternal birth of the divine Son takes place unceasingly, but does not take place within myself? And, what good is it to me if Mary is full of grace if I am not also full of grace? What good is it to me for the Creator to give birth to his Son if I do not also give birth to him in my time and my culture? This, then, is the fullness of time: when the Son of God is begotten in us.

## Questions to Ponder

- Consider an event or issue around which you are anxious. What projects or preparations might you undertake to turn that anxiety into greater joy?
- Regardless of your age and gender, imagine that you are pregnant (if you are not already!). What personal routines would you need to seriously alter to make room for another life?

## Prayer

O God of new life, who desires to give birth within each one of us, awaken us to the expectations and responsibilities that go with being your faithful people. Renew our perspective when we struggle to see your hand in new beginnings. Amen.

# Day 26: Thursday

## Putting Broken Lives Back Together

Revelation 21:1-5

> 🗨 *Key Verse:* The one who was seated on the throne said, "See, I am making all things new." Revelation 21:5

"Humpty Dumpty" is one of the best-known nursery rhymes in the English-speaking world. Comprised of only one verse, about an egg-shaped creature that falls off a wall, the poem's four simple lines are known the world over.

Writer Vic Pentz decided to play around with this traditional story of Humpty Dumpty and offer up his own variation. In Pentz's version, after the king's horses and king's men cannot manage to put Humpty Dumpty back together, the king himself shows up. "It is I—your King! I have powers greater than those of my horses and men who failed to put you together again. Be at peace. I am here to help."

Humpty's response is anything but welcoming. "Leave me alone. I've gotten used to this new way of life. I kind of like it." When the king persists in his effort to help, even returning a week later, Humpty hunkers down with a fatalistic mind-set: "Look, leave me alone, will you? I've just seen my psychiatrist and he assures me that I'm doing a fine job of coping with my environment as it is. A man has to deal with life as it comes. I'm a realist."

We could plug our own name into Vic Pentz's version of Humpty Dumpty. Eliminate the trip to the psychiatrist's office, if that doesn't seem to apply. On the whole, we know what it's like to get used to a way of life that works for us, even if it's broken. Pick whatever form of brokenness you wish. If it stays a part of life too long, we ritualize it. That's when we often employ the line "Leave me alone."

Enter Revelation, actually the second-to-the-last chapter of the book of Revelation. Here at the end of the Bible, God speaks of a gift that will be given to all. It is the gift of new life where old things will become brand new. Even tears from the worst of grief will dry up and be no more. All the unspeakable pain and suffering in our lives will come to a decisive end. The Lord of hosts will reign.

How will this renewal happen? According to the promise of Revelation, God will make a home in our hearts and will dwell with us. It is exactly what the king elects to do in Vic Pentz's version of Humpty Dumpty. He sits down in the broken shards of Humpty's life and helps him put life back together again. We Christians have a better story than this little nursery rhyme. It's called the gospel. Jesus is the main character, and his whole purpose is to dwell *with us* in grace and truth.

## Questions to Ponder

· List some of the broken places in your life, emotionally, spiritually, and relationally. What might you do with God to break out of the rut of stubbornness and self-pity that often characterizes long-term brokenness?

· If your spiritual life were to experience an "extreme makeover," to borrow a phrase from a television program, what would be the features of this makeover?

## Prayer

Grant that we may serve you in newness of life, O God, especially when we are crushed and broken. Come dwell with us. Abide with us. Teach us your best name—Immanuel, God with us. Amen.

## Day 27: Friday

### Starting Anew

2 Corinthians 5:16-21

> *Key Verse:* If anyone is in Christ, there is a new creation: everything old has passed away; see, everything has become new! 2 Corinthians 5:17

One of the tales from Thomas Edison's storied life happened on a cold night in December 1914. In his West Orange, New Jersey, laboratory—or "factory of inventions" as it might well have been called—a spectacular blaze broke out. It was a sudden combustion of dangerous materials. The entire film room, with all its packing compounds, celluloid for film, and other flammable chemicals, quickly turned the place into an inferno. Fire companies from eight surrounding towns came to battle the flames.

As the fire tore through the roof structure, the inventor's son, Charles, went frantically looking for his father. When he finally found him, his father was calmly watching the fire on the other side of the plant. His hair blowing in the wind, and with bright flames reflecting off his face, Thomas Edison was seeing two million dollars' worth of assets disappear in minutes.

"My heart ached for him," said Charles. "Here he was, sixty-seven years old, and virtually everything he had worked for was going up in flames. When he saw me, he shouted, 'Charles! Where's your mother?' When I told him I didn't know, he said, 'Find her. Bring her here. She'll never see anything like this as long as she lives.'"

The next morning, looking over the ruins of his factory, the elder Edison noted, "There is great value in disaster. All our mistakes are burned up. Thank God we can start anew." Three weeks later, Edison delivered the first phonograph.

This is a wonderful story, with an incredibly positive attitude growing out of loss. But is this what it means to be a *new creation* in the Christian sense of Scripture? When the apostle Paul writes of everything old passing away and all things becoming new, could he be intending the same expression as Thomas Edison—optimistic words spoken after suffering great loss? Probably not.

Newness in the Christian life is connected with being "in Christ." Paul repeats this phrase many times over to drive home the deep bond that results from believers who trust the entirety of their lives to Christ. To invest everything we are and all that matters to us in the promises of Christ is to see our circumstances in a whole new light. Being a new creature in Christ is comprised of more than a good attitude. It is larger than some positive thinking about adverse conditions. To be completely *in Christ* is to be unable to distinguish the Lord's priorities from our desires.

A life embedded in Christ is one that can enjoy daily renewal, not as an attitude, a positive outlook, or even a decision of the mind, but as a gift of divine grace.

### Questions to Ponder

- Think of some object in your house that you have repaired multiple times, or some puzzle you have repeatedly tried to solve. What feature of your personality allows you to keep starting over?
- What exactly would it require of you and your closest family and friends if all of you spent one week refusing to look at other people "from a human point of view" (2 Corinthians 5:16)?

### Prayer

O God of inventive genius, who inspires us to create and imagine, do something for us that we cannot do entirely by ourselves. Make us new creatures *in Christ*. Amen.

## Day 28: Saturday

### Unknown Next Steps

Isaiah 43:15-19

> 🔲 *Key Verse:* Do not remember the former things, or consider the things of old. I am about to do a new thing; now it springs forth, do you not perceive it? I will make a way in the wilderness and rivers in the desert. Isaiah 43:18-19

Several years ago, a 43-year-old Loyola University professor did something most of us would never consider trying. He set a world record for consecutive hours on a roller coaster. With a specially padded seat that would allow him to sleep while riding, and a small toilet outfitted for his little car, Mr. Rodriguez spent 195 hours riding a roller coaster in a German amusement park. If you do the math, he traveled more than eight straight days spinning, diving, climbing, and, well . . . probably getting sick.

Talk about going in circles or having your day pre-defined for you! This man's journey was the epitome of sameness. Record-breaking as his journey might have been, it bears little resemblance to the unpredictable next steps that people of faith must walk. The entire story of faith in the Bible is one of people on the move, undertaking a pilgrimage of adventurous proportions.

Slavery in Egypt provided plenty of sameness. Every day looked like the one before and the one after. Brick-making under Middle Eastern sunshine is hot and monotonous. It took Moses's urging, cajoling, pushing, and prodding to get the people of Israel to appreciate the new life over the next horizon. It would indeed be a brand-new life, shaped by one brand-new day after another. Anyone who has spent any time in the desert knows that there are few paths when traversing the vast open spaces of blowing sand. Someone would have to help the Hebrew people make a way, and this someone would turn out to be God.

One of the greatest journey prayers ever written is this one by Thomas Merton (1915–1968) that speaks to our unknown next steps:

My Lord God, I have no idea where I am going. I do not see the road ahead of me. I cannot know for certain where it will end. Nor do I really know myself, and the fact that I think that I am following your will does not mean that I am actually doing so. But I believe that the desire to please you does in fact please you. And I hope I have that desire in all that I am doing. I hope that I will never do anything apart from that desire. And I know that if I do this you will lead me by the right road.

## Questions to Ponder

- If you drive a car, consider taking different routes to and from church, or to and from other destinations, during these weeks of Advent. Try to notice sights along the way that you never knew were in the neighborhood or along the route. Think about these sights and some of what God or the people behind them might say to your life.
- Think of a time when you were lost. How did you react or behave? Describe the strategies or coping mechanisms you used to find your way. What helpful advice would you give to someone else who is lost?

## Prayer

Dear God, some mornings I have no idea where I am going. I put one foot in front of the other and hope it leads toward meaning. Show me a way, or at the very least, reveal yourself to me through the people and moments of this day. Amen.

# Bible Studies

## Bible Study: Week 1

### Renew Our Stories

| | |
|---|---|
| Genesis 3:8-13, 21 | Luke 2:1-20 |
| Genesis 50:15-21 | 1 Corinthians 1:18-25 |

Every day God is renewing our stories, truly making us new. Throughout the Bible, God acts over and over again to call people back, offering forgiveness and new life. As Christians, we see this most clearly in Jesus Christ, who takes all our sad, broken, tattered stories with him to the cross, and in return gives us his story of resurrection.

1. Early on in the garden of Eden, God says disobedience will mean death. Read Genesis 3:8-9 and 21, and discuss how God works to create a new story after Adam and Eve disobeyed. Recall an occasion from your life or a loved one's life or current events, in which a hopeful story emerged from a situation that initially seemed hopeless. How do you see God at work in this story?

---

---

---

2. Joseph's story, told in Genesis 37–50, has many twists and turns. Sold by his brothers to a group of traders, he becomes a servant in Egypt to one of Pharaoh's officials. Later he is thrown in prison. His ability to interpret dreams eventually gets him out of prison and into a high government position. During a widespread famine, Joseph's brothers end up coming to Egypt to find food. Of course, they expect Joseph to carry a grudge against them. Read

about his response in Genesis 50:15-21. As you think about your life, how has God been working for good in your story?

_____

_____

_____

3. Pay attention to what the angels, the shepherds, and Mary do with the story as you read Luke 2:1-20. What do you do with this story? How does this story renew your story and our story as a church?

_____

_____

_____

4. God chose to become absolutely vulnerable by entering the world as a child and going to the cross. Look at 1 Corinthians 1:18-25 and talk about how this weakness and foolishness, in the eyes of the world, shows God's power and wisdom. How is this a story of God's love?

_____

_____

_____

# Bible Study: Week 2

## Renew Our Days

*1855*

Ephesians 4:1-32                    Matthew 6:19-21, 25-34

*1863* Philippians 4:4-9            Mark 12:28-31

Our daily lives can easily become a daily grind of running around in circles or doing the same old things. But God makes all things new, including our days. Following Jesus and serving him in the world actively engages us in helping others. It changes what we put in our calendars, how we think about success, how we set our priorities, and where we put our passion and resources each day.

1.  Some families have a tradition of including new clothes in the gifts under the Christmas tree. After these gifts are unwrapped, there's a parade of trying things on to see how they fit. Read Ephesians 4:1-32. In the description of the new life in Christ, underline what would be new for you. What "altering" needs to take place so that you can put on more of Christ's nature?

_____

_____

_____

2.  We often dwell on our worries and not on God's blessings. Read Philippians 4:4-9. What could you give thanks for or rejoice about today? What would it look like or sound like for you to tell God about all your wants and needs today, and to do that with joy and thanksgiving? How would focusing on the good renew your days?

_____

_____

_____

3. Read Matthew 6:19-21. Daily life can become consumed with acquiring more and more material things. Name some of your "treasures on earth" and "treasures in heaven." What would happen if your days were filled with storing up more "treasures in heaven"?

_____

_____

_____

4. Read Matthew 6:25-34. Based on this text, write a list of priorities for one day. Discuss your reactions to this list. What could you or your congregation do to relieve the worries of someone in need of food, clothing, or shelter?

_____

_____

_____

5. Read the commandment from Jesus in Mark 12:28-31. The word _love_ here is not a thought or a feeling. It's an action, a way of life, something we do. What difference does this make? How does this commandment give purpose to your days?

_____

_____

_____

# Bible Study: Week 3

## Renew Our Spirits

John 3:1-16

Ephesians 3:14-21; 4:17-24

Philippians 1:27-30

Titus 3:1-7

Revelation 21:1-4, 22-27

God renews our spirits daily in the forgiveness of sin. We already live in the new age of Christ, experiencing life in the Spirit. And we look forward in hope, not only to renewal each day, but also to God's final renewal of our spirits on the other side of death. Then we will be with Christ forever, clad in a new garment of eternal life.

1. What phrases, images, Bible verses, or hymns come to mind when you hear the words "renew our spirits"?

_____

_____

2. Read John 3:1-16. Rebirth or total renewal of our very selves comes from God. In what ways is the Advent season an opportunity to pray for and expect that God will renew us?

_____

_____

3. Read Ephesians 3:14-21; 4:17-24. These verses speak of Christ's indwelling (3:17) and the Christian's "new self" (4:24). How have you been "strengthened in

your inner being with power through his Spirit" (3:16) and "renewed in the spirit of your minds" (4:23)?

_start here_

4. Read Philippians 1:27-30. Renewal is more than an individual matter; we have a shared spirit in the church. Paul wants the Philippian believers to stand firm in one spirit and to strive side by side with one mind for the faith of the gospel. How does renewal by the Spirit call us to oneness in the church in spite of our differences?

5. Read Titus 3:1-7. Renewal is given to us in baptism, the water of rebirth (3:5). It is the work of the Holy Spirit (3:5-6), setting us into right relations with God through Christ by grace (3:7). What kinds of renewal come to mind when you see someone baptized?

6. Read Revelation 21:1-4, 22-27, which speaks about God's final work of renewal. The Savior born at Christmas is the lamb and the lamp of the eternal city. Why is Advent a good time to remember God's final promises? How does your view of the babe of Bethlehem expand when reading this passage?

# Bible Study: Week 4

## Renew Our Ways

Matthew 5:43-48

Psalm 103:1-5

Matthew 16:24-26

Galatians 2:20

Luke 2:22-32

Newness in the Christian life is connected with being "in Christ": "So if anyone is in Christ, there is a new creation: everything old has passed away; see, everything has become new!" (2 Corinthians 5:17). To invest everything we are and all that matters to us in the promises of Christ is to see our circumstances in a whole new light. To be completely *in Christ* is to be unable to distinguish the Lord's priorities from our desires.

1. When Jesus tried to get fresh thinking from his followers, he often said, "You have heard that it was said . . . but I say to you." Therapists in our day sometimes use the phrase "Up until now . . ." as a way of helping clients distinguish future behaviors from past ones. Read Matthew 5:43-48. Make a list of people you find difficult to love. What do they have in common? What attitudinal and behavioral changes are required of you for a different future?

_____

_____

_____

2. Read Matthew 16:24-26. As a loon dives deeper in a lake, its resurfacing point becomes more unpredictable. So, too, the more deeply we "lose ourselves"

in Christ, the greater the chance we will come up a more wholly new person. Talk with others about what it really means to "lose your (way of?) life."

3. When the elderly Simeon got to hold the infant Christ, the experience brought unparalleled consolation and renewed peace to his life. Read Luke 2:22-32 and explore this passage. Imagine opening a preschool, daycare, and family play area in a retirement or nursing home complex. What features would you incorporate into the design and staffing?

4. Read Psalm 103:1-5. The ancient Hebrews knew that an eagle sheds and re-grows its feathers annually. Thus, the *renewal* of life and strength in people became connected with images of this bird. What material things or behaviors might you shed from your life this Advent to be renewed?

5. The allegedly "new and improved model" at the store or car dealership often proves to be the same old thing with some cosmetic changes. Study and pray over Galatians 2:20 contemplatively. Exploring your inner life with great honesty, what in your outlook and daily habits needs more than a cosmetic tweak or superficial readjustment?

# Activities

# Week 1: Renew Our Stories

### Faith Flag Banner (week 1 of 4)

Build your own Faith Flag Banner over the next four weeks. Hang it over a mantel, in a doorway, or along a stairway banister in your home.

Materials needed: length of twine or cord, scissors, assorted papers or fabrics, ruler, markers, thin cardboard for a pattern or template, glue sticks or a sewing machine and thread

Time required: 15 minutes

1. Talk about the season of Advent and the four-week "renewing" you and your family will focus on during this season. Talk about the word *renew* and what it means to you, inviting everyone to add their thoughts and ideas. Spend a few minutes telling about how God renews our stories through love, forgiveness, other people, the Bible, the church, baptism, and so on. What kinds of symbols, art, or words can reflect this?

2. Decide where you will hang the Faith Flag Banner throughout the four weeks. Measure and cut the twine or cord to fit that space, allowing extra length for attaching each end.

3. Draw a diamond shape on the cardboard, making sure that when you fold the diamond in half (point to point) it will make a triangle. You will want your completed triangles to be at least 6 inches (15.24 centimeters) from the folded edge to the opposite point. (See figure 1.)

4. Let everyone choose their favorite papers or fabrics for diamond shapes. Cut enough diamond shapes to fill the twine or cord when folded, with some space left on each end. Work on one-fourth of the diamond shapes each week.

5. Fold this week's diamonds in half and decorate both sides of the faith flags with markers or cut-out paper or fabric scraps of words, symbols, or designs. Glue or sew the pieces to the flags.

6. Slide the folded edge of the flags over the twine or cord and glue or sew to secure them. (See figure 2.)

7. Hang the Faith Flag Banner until you work on it again in the second week of Advent.

8. Gather together as a family near or under this banner each time you meet, daily or weekly, for Advent devotions or a time of prayer and praise. Share family stories that tell about God making all things new.

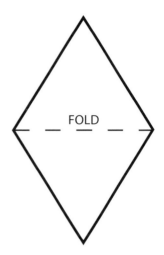

Figure 1

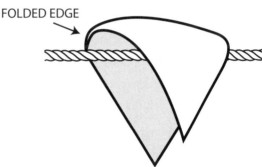

Figure 2

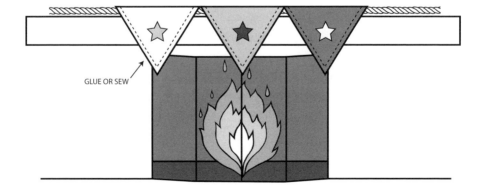

## Pinecone Fire Starters

There's nothing like a cozy fire in the fireplace on a cold winter night! And it's even better to sit by a fire and tell a story or two.

Materials needed: block of paraffin wax, old candles or crayons; muffin tin, paper baking cups, string, pinecones, scissors, double boiler (a saucepan and a large metal can that will fit inside), spoon, water

Time required: 20–30 minutes

Safety first: Adults should always be involved in the creative process when using a stove and candle wax.

1. Cut one length of string for each pinecone, approximately 6 to 8 inches (15.24 to 20.32 centimeters) long, depending on the size of your cones.

2. Put baking cups into the muffin tin and coil a section of the string in the bottom of each.

3. Choose pinecones that will fit snugly into the paper baking cups, and set a pinecone on top of the string in each.

4. Wrap the string loosely around the cone, leaving a few inches (about 7.62 centimeters) hanging out over the side of the paper baking cup.

5. Fill the saucepan half full of water and set the metal can in it. Make sure the water level is low enough that water does not spill out of the pan.

6. Put the paraffin or wax into the can and turn the heat on low. Watch carefully and keep stirring.

7. When the wax is melted, pour it carefully into each baking cup, filling each cup about halfway up the pinecone.

8. Let the wax harden, and remove the fire starters from the muffin tin.

9. Store fire starters in a basket near a fireplace, or wrap them up as a gift for a family member or friend.

10. To start a fire in a fireplace, set a fire starter on top of kindling, light the string, and watch the glow begin!

## Marbleized Stars

*Where is the child who has been born king of the Jews? For we observed his star at its rising, and have come to pay him homage. Matthew 2:2*

The star of Bethlehem is a sign and symbol of the story of God's love for us in the gift of Jesus.

Materials needed: wooden or papier-mâché stars or thin wood or heavy cardboard, assorted colors of spray paint, bucket, water, rubber gloves, newspaper, paper clips, string, clothes hanger

Time required: 15 minutes

Safety first: Adults should always be involved when using spray paint. Make sure your work area is well ventilated.

1. Purchase wooden or papier-mâché stars in a craft store, or cut your own star shapes from thin wood or heavy cardboard.

2. Make a hole in one point of the star and slip one end of a paper clip through it. Attach a piece of string to the other end of the paper clip.

3. Fill the bucket half full of water and set it on newspaper. Spray three or more colors of spray paint into the water—it will swirl into a cool design. Metallic spray paint adds a nice touch!

4. Put on rubber gloves and hold the star by the string. Lower the star into the water until it is totally submerged.

5. Carefully pull the star out of the water and see the marbleized design that appears on both sides!

6. Tie the stars to the clothes hanger and hang over newspaper to dry.

## Spell-It-Out Frame

Use game-piece letter tiles to make a family photo frame! What story does your photo tell about your family and how you spend time together?

Materials needed: simple plastic or wooden picture frame, game-piece letter tiles, white glue, family photo

Time required: 20 minutes

1. Talk with your family about a special message to spell out on a family photo frame. For example, you could spell the names of the people in your family, or use a phrase such as "Family fun," or even something about where the photo was taken, such as "Camping together."

2. Sort out the letter tiles to create your words and glue them along one or more sides of the frame.

3. When the glue dries, insert your family photo and display for everyone to enjoy!

4. If you have fun with this project, you might want to collect more letter tiles and make letter tile frames for Christmas gifts.

## Photo Favorites

*Every picture tells a story.*

Take a special photo and turn it into a unique favorite!

Materials needed: favorite photo of someone you love, a pet, or a simple landscape; copy machine or scanner, heavy white paper (like watercolor paper) or heavy black paper, masking tape, sharp scissors, glue, paper clips, pushpins, tapestry sewing needle and black or colored embroidery thread, glue stick

Time required: 45 minutes or more

1. Make a copy of the photo image so you can preserve the original. Decide if you will make a stitched version or a silhouette version of your image. Have family members take turns with each of the steps for these photo ideas.

2. For the stitched version, tape the photo onto the heavy white paper along the edges. Use the pushpin to punch holes outlining the image, and add holes for facial features, hair, clothing, ears and noses of pets, and so forth.

3. Once you have punched the holes you will need, remove the taped photo. Use the sewing needle and embroidery thread to sew through the holes. This is like the lacing cards often used by young children. You can use a simple running stitch or a backstitch for your design.

4. When your stitching is done, tie a knot in the thread on the back side of the paper and cut off the thread. Trim to fit a frame and hang to enjoy!

5. For a silhouette version of your image, follow the first step and photocopy the image. Tape the image to the heavy black paper and cut around the outer edge of the image to make a silhouette shape.

6. Center and glue the black silhouette to the white paper, trim to fit the frame, and enjoy!

# Week 2: Renew Our Days

## Faith Flag Banner (week 2 of 4)

Add more flags in this second week of building your Faith Flag Banner.

Materials needed: diamond shapes cut last week, scissors, assorted papers or fabrics, ruler, markers, glue sticks or a sewing machine and thread

Time required: 15 minutes

1. If you did not begin this activity last week, look back to pages 82–83 to find out what steps to follow to prepare.

2. Talk about how God has been growing your faith this past week. What did everyone learn? How did God renew your stories, especially your faith stories?

3. Spend a few minutes talking about how God renews our days. What kinds of symbols, art, or words can reflect this?

4. Work on the faith flags for this week. Fold the diamonds in half and decorate both sides with markers or cut-out paper or fabric scraps of words, symbols, or designs. Glue or sew the pieces to the flags.

5. Slide the folded edge of the flags over the twine and glue or sew to secure them.

6. Hang the Faith Flag Banner until you work on it again in the third week of Advent.

7. Gather together as a family near or under this banner for daily or weekly Advent devotions or a time of prayer and praise. Share thoughts and stories about how God makes each day new.

## Pocket Praise Stones

*O LORD, you are our Father; we are the clay, and you are our potter; we are all the work of your hand. Isaiah 64:8*

Some people carry a "worry stone" in their pockets each day and rub it when they feel anxious or worried. Make a clay stone to carry in your pocket, and use it as a reminder to pray and praise God each day for renewing and refreshing us!

Materials needed: saucepan and spoon, 1 cup (240 ml) baking soda, ½ cup (120 ml) cornstarch, ¾ cup (180 ml) cold water, damp towel, cutting board, food coloring, paint or nail polish (optional)

Time required: 15 minutes to make the clay, 10 minutes for the clay to cool, 5 minutes to make the stones

Safety first: Adults should always participate with children when doing an activity that requires the use of a stove or oven.

1. Measure the dry ingredients into the saucepan and mix together.

2. Add the water slowly to the pan, stirring to mix as you pour.

3. Set the pan over medium heat and stir until the mixture begins to boil.

4. Stir out any lumps or clumps and continue cooking until the dough is the consistency of mashed potatoes.

5. When the dough has formed one large ball, turn it out onto the damp kitchen towel on the cutting board. Cool.

6. When the clay is cool to the touch, dust a work surface with a little cornstarch and begin kneading the clay until it is pliable.

7. If you like, add a few drops of food coloring as you knead the clay, or you can leave the clay white and paint it once it has hardened.

8. Pinch off small pieces of clay and roll into balls. Set the balls on the work surface and press down on them with your thumbs to make an indented stone.

9. After about 12 hours of drying time, paint the finished stones with acrylic paint or even nail polish for a little shine.

## Tea Bag Scripture Tags

*Pleasant words are like a honeycomb, sweetness to the soul and health to the body.*
*Proverbs 16:24*

Ah, there is nothing more comforting or renewing after a long day than a cup of hot tea! Make your own scripture tags to add to tea time.

Materials needed: Bible, tea bags with strings, small scraps of paper, scissors, glue or glue stick; fine-tipped pens or computer, printer, and paper

Time required: 10 minutes

1. Take the tea bags out of their envelopes, making sure to keep the tags attached to the tea-bag strings.

2. Cut assorted colors and designs of paper scraps into small squares, rectangles, or other shapes, large enough to cover the original tea bag tag. You will need two pieces the same size for each tea bag. Put glue on one piece of paper, then sandwich the original tag between that paper and the second piece.

3. Press and let dry.

4. Do this with a number of tea bags and set aside.

5. Use your Bible to find verses that are especially meaningful to use on the tags. You could also use words of encouragement or even a prayer.

6. For each tea bag, cut one more piece of paper just a bit smaller than the first two you cut. Write your message on this piece of paper. Another option: use a computer and printer to print out many messages on one sheet of paper, then cut them apart.

7. Glue the messages to one side of the tea bag tags you have set aside. Let dry.

8. Create your own tags for an entire box of tea bags, or slip a few bags with scripture tags into the tea canister to surprise someone. These are fun to use for your own family, but also nice to share as gifts.

9. Now sit back with a cup of warm tea—and don't forget the honey!

## Clothespin Message Holders

Make Clothespin Message Holders with an extra touch for this season of Advent.

Materials needed: wooden clip clothespins, acrylic paints, brushes, newspaper, fine-tipped black markers, self-stick magnet strips

Time required: 15 minutes, not counting paint-drying time

1. Cover your work surface with newspaper.

2. Let everyone paint clothespins with their favorite acrylic colors. Acrylic paints dry quickly, so it is best to use them.

3. Once the paint dries, let everyone in the family use the markers to personalize their clothespins with words, names, or designs such as squiggles, stripes, or spots. Some might even want to spell out a message or a name by writing one letter on each clothespin, or use symbols for the season of Advent.

4. Stick magnets on the back sides of the clothespins.

5. Write messages of love and encouragement to one another during Advent, and use your new Clothespin Message Holders to post your messages on the refrigerator, a metal cabinet, or other unexpected places around your home!

## Renewed and Reused: Magazine Strip Coasters

Renew . . . reuse . . . recycle. These words are familiar to those who care for God's world. Make coasters for glasses and cups using magazine strips, and test out your own renewing touch!

Materials needed: used magazine pages, scissors, glue sticks, wax paper, decoupage medium or mixture of half white glue and half water, foam brushes

Time required: 45 minutes

1. Choose pages from used magazines that have colors you like or have simple black and white text. You will need about 12 regular-size pages to make a coaster that will fit the base of a soda pop can.

2. Make each coaster on a sheet of wax paper so you don't get decoupage medium on your work surface.

3. Lay the colorful side of a magazine page face down and start folding along the longest edge. Make ½-inch (1.27 centimeters) folds over and over the length of the page until you have one long strip.

4. Press the folds along the edge of the paper so they are tight, and run the glue stick along the outer edges to keep them secure.

5. Hold one end of the strip and fold it tightly into a circle.

6. Roll the paper around this center circle until you have a round roll that fits tightly together. Use a foam brush to spread a decoupage medium (or white glue and water mixture) on the rolled section so it stays attached and does not unroll.

7. Continue to fold and roll magazine pages, rolling around the middle circle until you reach the size you want.

8. Add the decoupage medium as needed to cover the paper rolls, keeping them tight together. Once you have reached the coaster size you want, use the foam brush to coat the top and bottom of the coaster, letting the decoupage medium soak into the paper. This helps to seal the paper against moisture from cans, bottles, or glasses.

9. Let dry completely and enjoy!

# Week 3: Renew Our Spirits

## Faith Flag Banner (week 3 of 4)

Add more flags during this third week of building your Faith Flag Banner.

Materials needed: diamond shapes, scissors, assorted papers or fabrics, ruler, markers, glue sticks or a sewing machine and thread

Time required: 15 minutes

1. If you did not begin this activity previously, look back to pages 82–83 to find out what steps to follow to prepare.

2. Talk about how God has been growing your faith this past week. What did everyone learn? How did God make each day new?

3. Spend a few minutes talking about how God renews our spirits. What kinds of symbols, art, or words can reflect this?

4. Work on the faith flags for this week. Fold the diamonds in half and decorate both sides with markers or cut-out paper or fabric scraps of words, symbols, or designs. Glue or sew the pieces to the flags.

5. Slide the folded edge of the flags over the twine and glue or sew to secure them.

6. Hang the Faith Flag Banner until you work on it again in the fourth week of Advent.

7. Gather together as a family near or under this banner for daily or weekly Advent devotions or a time of prayer and praise. Share thoughts and stories about how God makes our spirits new.

## An Early Sign of New Life

Flowers blooming will renew your spirits every time you see them! During this darkest time of the year, it is good to plan ahead for the new life that spring brings. Planting bulbs to bloom in midwinter makes a great family activity and a fun gift to share with people you know.

Materials needed: one or more types of spring bulbs, such as hyacinths, crocus, amaryllis, or paper whites; small pots, plastic lids, potting soil, trowel or small shovel, newspaper, water, small pebbles (optional)

Time required: 15 minutes, not counting shopping or growing time

1. Cover your work surface with newspaper.

2. Fill the pots three-quarters full of potting soil, then use the trowel or shovel to make a large hole in the center of the soil.

3. Place several bulbs into the soil, a few inches (about 7.62 centimeters) down into the hole. Press a bit of dirt around the bulbs to make them secure.

4. Water lightly after putting a plastic lid under your pot so water doesn't ruin a tabletop or windowsill.

5. Most purchased bulbs will have been "cool treated" before you bring them home, and will begin to grow quickly if placed in a sunny window. If you are using bulbs that have not been cool treated, you may want to put the pots into a cool dark place (like a garage or basement) for a week or so, before placing them in a sunny spot to begin the growth process.

## Pretzel Dips

A little bit salty and a little bit sweet makes a yummy, tasty treat!

Materials needed: microwave oven, pretzels (sticks or regular), your favorite variety of melting chocolate, wooden spoon, tongs, glass mixing bowl, baking sheet, parchment paper

Time required: 10–15 minutes

**Safety first:** The bowl and wooden spoon may be hot when removed from the microwave oven. Adults should always be part of the cooking process when young children are involved.

1. Line the baking sheet with a piece of parchment paper.

2. Follow instructions on the melting chocolate on how to use it in a microwave oven with a glass bowl.

3. Stir the chocolate thoroughly as it melts, then use tongs to pick up the pretzels and dip them into the chocolate.

4. Shake any excess chocolate drippings back into the bowl, and then lay the pretzels on the parchment paper to set.

5. Once the chocolate has hardened, take a bite!

6. These treats are easy to make and fun to share with teachers, postal workers, or other people you interact with on a daily basis.

## Prayer Central

*Let my prayer be counted as incense before you, and the lifting up of my hands as an evening sacrifice. Psalm 141:2*

Create a Prayer Central for your family during this Advent time!

**Materials needed:** refrigerator, bulletin board, or other central message place in your home; basket or box, glue stick, large sheet of paper, scissors, alphabet stamps, ink pads; paper or letters cut from magazines, newspaper, or other print items

**Time required:** 5–10 minutes

1. Gather the print materials or alphabet stamps, ink pads, and paper, and cut out or stamp letters, words, and phrases of all sorts. Include the names of people you know, places, and common themes such as hunger, peace, love, or God's word. Cut these out and keep them in the basket or box near your Prayer Central location.

2. Talk about your Prayer Central as a place for everyone to add their prayers of thanksgiving, requests, and praise.

3. Mount the large piece of paper on the refrigerator or other location, then let everyone glue the letters and words, graffiti style, to the paper to add their prayers.

4. Encourage all members of the family to contribute, helping the nonreaders and nonwriters to choose their letters or having them draw their prayers. Throughout the weeks ahead, keep this location central as a reminder that you can raise these prayers to God.

## Word Cube Key Rings

Use letter cubes or beads from a craft store to make key ring reminders of God's renewing grace!

**Materials needed:** one key ring per person, letter cubes or beads from a craft store, heavy twine or leather cords, scissors

**Time required:** 10 minutes

1. Talk about the faith words that have been part of your Advent conversations. What words come to mind when you think about how God renews your stories, your days, and your spirits? Use these words with your key rings.

2. Have fun laying out the letter cubes or beads to spell the words you have chosen.

3. Once you know how many cubes or beads you need, cut the twine or leather cord three times as long as each word will be.

4. Fold the cord in half and attach it to the key ring by slipping the cord ends through the loop and pulling it tight. Now thread the letter cubes onto the cord, one letter at a time, tying a knot between each letter.

5. When the word is complete, tie a square knot to secure the beads to the ring, and cut off any excess cord.

# Week 4: Renew Our Ways

### Faith Flag Banner (week 4 of 4)

Add the final flags during this fourth week of building your Faith Flag Banner.

Materials needed: diamond shapes, scissors, assorted papers or fabrics, ruler, markers, glue sticks or a sewing machine and thread

Time required: 15 minutes

1. If you did not begin this project activity previously, look back to pages 82–83 to find out what steps to follow to prepare.

2. Talk about how God has been growing your faith this past week. What did everyone learn? What are some of the ways that God renewed your spirits?

3. Spend a few minutes talking about how God renews our ways. What kinds of symbols, art, or words can reflect this?

4. Work on the faith flags for this week. Fold the diamonds in half and decorate both sides with markers or cut-out paper or fabric scraps of words, symbols, or designs. Glue or sew the pieces to the triangles.

5. Slide the folded edge of the flags over the twine and glue or sew to secure them.

6. Hang the Faith Flag Banner.

7. Gather together as a family near or under this banner for daily or weekly Advent devotions or a time of prayer and praise. Share thoughts and stories about how God makes our ways new.

## Stuffed Stockings

Warm new socks stuffed with personal-care items and special treats are welcome gifts for a local shelter or food bank in your community.

Materials needed: several pairs of new heavy athletic-type socks; small personal-care items such as hand sanitizer, travel-size containers of toothpaste, shampoo, soap, and so on; granola bars, packs of gum, candy bars, meal coupons for local restaurants, rolls of dimes or quarters; gift tags, markers

Time required: 15 minutes stocking stuffing time, not counting shopping time

1. Shop together for socks and personal items, if possible. This could have a big impact on family members.

2. Roll one of each pair of athletic socks as small as possible and stuff it down into the toe of the second sock. Then fill the socks with the other items you have collected, adding some fun things like gum or candy on top.

3. As you are stuffing the socks, talk about how blessed you are to have the items you need such as food, clothing, and a warm home, and how you and your family can be a blessing to others by sharing these socks and their stuffing!

4. Go together to a local shelter or food bank to donate your Stuffed Stockings.

5. Consider ways to continue sharing with this facility year-round by donating items, time, or money.

## All God's Critters

Good stewardship means caring for all of God's creation. Make simple bird-seed ornaments to feed the critters that visit your yard or balcony during the winter months.

Materials needed: day-old sliced sandwich bread, peanut butter, plastic knives, bird seed, large cookie cutters, baking sheets, straws, string or twine, scissors

Time required: 20 minutes

1. Have everyone choose a favorite cookie cutter and press it into a piece of bread.

2. Use the straws to poke a hole in the top of the bread shape.

3. Pour bird seed onto the baking tray and spread it out evenly.

4. Spread an even layer of peanut butter on one side of the bread shape and press it into the bird seed. The seeds will stick to the peanut butter.

5. Now turn the bread shape over and spread a layer of peanut butter on that side. Follow the same process of pressing the bread into the bird seed.

6. When both sides have a nice coating of bird seed, tie a length of cord or twine through the hole in the bread.

7. Hang the bird-seed ornaments in a tree or from a bird feeder and watch God's critters come to enjoy them!

## Roll 'em!

Spend some quality family time playing this variation of a fun dice game.

Materials needed: one die, paper, pencils

Time required: 20–30 minutes

1. The goal of this game is to be the first one to complete the figure of an angel.

2. Each person will roll the die for a number, and the number corresponds to the particular body part of the angel they will need to draw on the paper.

3. The body of the angel needs to be drawn before the other parts are added, so the first person to roll a 6 will be the first one to draw.

4. Once the body has been drawn, the other parts of the angel can be added in any order. If someone rolls a number that has already been drawn, they skip a turn and pass the die on.

5. Body parts and corresponding numbers are:

> 6 = body
> 5 = mouth
> 4 = halo
> 3 = eyes
> 2 - wings
> 1 = head

6. After you have finished the angel, adapt this dice game for other parts of the Christmas story. What about the shepherds or sheep? Wise Men? Mary or Joseph? The stable where Jesus was born, and the manger?

7. If you decide to add these adaptations, you can use a larger sheet of paper and create an entire nativity scene to add to your home's Christmas decorations.

## Stained-Glass Foil Ornaments

Simple household materials make beautiful "stained glass" ornaments to hang on your Christmas tree or to use as Christmas cards or gift tags for friends and family.

Materials needed: newspaper, roll of aluminum foil, nontoxic permanent markers in assorted colors, items with raised designs to trace (optional), colorful construction paper, paper hole punch, thin cord or twine, glue stick, painting shirts or art smocks

Time required: 20–30 minutes

1. You will need a smooth surface to work on, as foil can tear with too much pressure on it.

2. Cover your work surface with newspaper. Protect your clothing with painting shirts or art smocks.

3. Cut the foil into the sizes you like. You might want to cut some traditional Gothic-style window shapes.

4. Decide on the designs you will draw on the foil, and use the permanent markers to color in the stained glass window spaces. Once the coloring is complete, use a permanent black marker to outline the shapes for definition.

5. Consider leaving some spaces on the foil without color to reflect and enhance the design.

6. If you have any household items that have a raised surface, an alternative design option is to lay the foil on top of the raised surface and press down gently, molding the foil slightly to the design. With this in place, use permanent markers to color the designs. Remove carefully and smooth out.

7. Cut construction paper to back and frame the foil design, gluing with a glue stick. For a card, make sure you use the correct size to fit into an envelope.

8. For an ornament, punch a hole in the top and loop a piece of cord or twine through for hanging on a Christmas tree or in a window.